Sunset

Reinvent Your Garden

Edited by Pamela Cornelison and the Editors of Sunset Books

MENLO PARK · CALIFORNIA

SUNSET BOOKS

VICE PRESIDENT, GENERAL MANAGER: Richard A. Smeby
VICE PRESIDENT, EDITORIAL DIRECTOR: Bob Doyle
PRODUCTION DIRECTOR: Lory Day
DIRECTOR OF OPERATIONS: Rosann Sutherland
SALES DEVELOPMENT DIRECTOR: Linda Barker
ART DIRECTOR: Vasken Guiragossian

STAFF FOR THIS BOOK

DEVELOPMENT/MANAGING EDITOR: Pamela Cornelison
ART DIRECTOR: Dorothy Marschall/Marschall Design
SENIOR EDITOR/GARDEN DESIGNER: Tom Wilhite
WRITERS: Marty Ross, Janet H. Sanchez
CONTRIBUTING EDITORS: Linda C. Askey, Steve Bender,
Kathleen N. Brenzel, John R. Dunmire, Philip Edinger,
Susan Lang, Steven R. Lorton, Jim McCausland,
Lauren Bonar Swezey, Peter O. Whiteley
PHOTO EDITOR/STYLIST: Cynthia Del Fava
ASSOCIATE PHOTO STYLIST: Jill Slater
COPY EDITOR: Rebecca LaBrum
ILLUSTRATOR: Beverley Bozarth Colgan
PROOFREADER: Christine Miklas
INDEXER: Pamela Evans
COMPUTER PRODUCTION: Maureen Spuhler, Linda Bouchard
PRODUCTION COORDINATOR: Danielle Javier

10 9 8 7 6 5 4 3 2 1

Printed in the United States

For additional copies of *Reinvent Your Garden* or any other
Sunset book, call 1-800-526-5111 or visit our web site at
www.sunsetbooks.com

COVER PHOTOGRAPHS: Marion Brenner (top left, bottom left,
right), Saxon Holt (left center)
COVER DESIGN: Vasken Guiragossian

The most noteworthy thing about gardeners is that they are always optimistic, always enterprising, and never satisfied. They always look forward to doing better than they have ever done before.

—VITA SACKVILLE-WEST

A pleasing garden is a collaboration between art and nature— between the gardener's skill and imagination and the unique character of the site, climate, and soil. Even in a small garden, nature presents unending possibilities, constantly branching out in new directions. Like nature's expression, your creative impulses must expand to capture the spirit of the garden and give it fresh meaning. That's what this book is all about. When you reinvent your garden, you're redefining and bringing out what experts call "the genius of the place."

A makeover doesn't have to throw the garden and your life into upheaval. Reinvent the whole yard, if you like—but do it one area at a time, starting in the front yard, on the back porch, or in a neglected corner. Above all, enjoy the process. Taken a step at a time, the projects here are easy and the materials are readily available and inexpensive.

Behind every garden makeover and project in this book is a team of talented and generous supporters: Karen Aitken Bernosky, Aitken & Associates Landscape Architecture; Roy Leporini, Peter Kiedrowski, Aptos Gardens; Bob Goode, Polly Joseph, the Pottery Planet; Lyngso Garden Materials; Monrovia Growers; Tiffany's Antiques; and Wegman's Nursery. A very special thanks to the generous people who invited us into their gardens and homes.

First Impressions

Front yards, typically the most public of all garden spaces, offer the perfect opportunity for a personal greeting and welcome. Reinvent your front garden to create a warm and lasting impression on all who enter.

FRESH IDEAS

Natural Connections

Usually narrow walk-through spaces, side yards are often left unattended and used to house utility cans and garden tools. But with a few good ideas, you can change that neglected space into a lush garden segue from front yard to back.

FRESH IDEAS

Personal Paradise

Whether spacious or postage-stamp size, backyards provide private outdoor living space for the gardener and family. Choose a favorite theme—from Mediterranean to meadow or Victorian to woodland—to turn your backyard into the paradise you've always wanted.

FRESH IDEAS

A Change of Scene

Gardens are the living frames of our lives, and, for many of us, they become central to our well-being. Each bright bloom, every artfully winding path, and each unique detail

First Impressions

Natural Connections

Personal Paradise

that make up our small corner of paradise help establish the mood of our days. ◐∿ But gardens are always changing: saplings grow into shade trees, plantings mature beyond the confines of their beds. We change, too. We explore new styles and try new plants and techniques. An interest in cooking inspires an herb garden; a move to a new home opens up opportunities to explore fresh gardening ideas. Children grow up, and where a swing set once stood, there's suddenly room for a cozy patio. ◐∿ The garden makeovers shown in the pages that follow grew from just such seeds of change. Most of them were small projects—some involved nothing more than a trip to a garden shop or home improvement center and a small investment in pots and plants. In others, trees were pruned, paths were laid, and plants were moved or replaced. In one garden, a storage area was transformed into a pleasant potting alcove. In another, a great view from a tiny balcony inspired an exciting container garden. ⟅⟆ In most projects, subtle changes were surprisingly effective. Others involved more collaboration between garden designers and gardeners. In every case—even where the possibilities were limited— ingenuity, creativity, and enthusiasm worked astonishing transformations. ⟅⟆ This book is designed to help you reinvent your own garden with confidence. You'll find ideas here for front yards and backyards, for challengingly narrow side yards, and for patios and balconies. A colored tab at the start of each project tells you whether you can "Do It Today" or "In a Weekend." A chapter of Snapshot Solutions gives 13 ideas for projects that can be done in any garden, anywhere. Step-by-step directions, photographs, and illustrations guide you through the process. In Great Plants for Makeovers, we list dozens of plants for tough situations. ⟅⟆ Reinventing a garden isn't difficult if you have a little help. You're already holding the guide. Just turn the page.

Urban Retreats

Snapshot Solutions

Great Plants

First Impressions

THE FRONT YARD is the gardener's opening statement, a gesture of greeting and welcome. It may be discreet, but it can still be stylish.

The main lines had already been drawn in this front yard. The low picket fence cleanly separated the garden from the street, and the lattice screen across the front of the house provided privacy—but the design of the garden between had become lost among overgrown plants. The crowded beds made working in the garden difficult: it was nearly impossible to tend one plant without stepping on another.

The new garden makes room for both plants and people. Evergreen dwarf viburnums anchor the front bed but will not outgrow it; silvery snow-in-summer and bright yellow coreopsis spread around them while roses echo the red door. A flagstone path allows easy access to the beds.

CHALLENGE

Overgrown, out-of-scale plantings gave the garden a hodge-podge look and dwarfed the small yard.

Routine maintenance was awkward at best, since there was no clear access to plantings.

SOLUTION

A refined design and new plants bring the garden in scale with the house and the available space.

A flagstone path now curves through the garden making it easy to tend all the plants.

BEFORE

Every time I go into a garden where the man or woman who owns it has a passionate love of the earth and of growing things, I find that I have come home.

—MARION CRAN

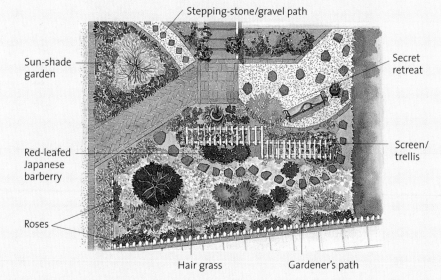

Stepping-stone/gravel path

Sun-shade garden

Secret retreat

Red-leafed Japanese barberry

Screen/ trellis

Roses

Hair grass

Gardener's path

A Welcome Wreath

THE VICTORIAN HOME'S front porch was charming, with Oriental-style balusters and a big parlor window right by the handsome original front door, but the entry looked severe compared to the garden around it. To dress it up and create a warm welcome, the owners borrowed a touch of the home's blue-gray trim for the front stairs and the banisters. A fern on a plant stand and an asymmetric arrangement of flashy pink bigleaf hydrangeas in pots on the stairs contribute to the Victorian style. The front door wears its curly willow wreath like a corsage.

TIP

FOR A DIFFERENT LOOK,

EMBELLISH THE WREATH

WITH DRIED DECORATIONS

SUCH AS LAVENDER SPRAYS,

ROSE HIPS, CHILI PEPPERS,

OR POPPY SEEDPODS.

Creating a Willow Wreath

1 Using only the curled parts of the willow branches, clip them into manageable lengths (12 to 16 inches long). Gather three lengths of willow in your hand and twine them around the wire ring. Gather three more lengths of willow and tuck the ends between the branches you already wrapped, starting at the mid-point of those branches. Continue twining branches around the wire until the entire ring is covered.

2 Insert stems of the flowers and dusty miller into the gaps between the branches. To finish, loosely twine a branch or two of willow over the flowers to enclose them slightly.

Air-drying Flowers

A blue-painted trellis in a matching pot makes a handsome drying rack for summer flowers such as lavender and hydrangeas. Center the trellis in the pot and pour gravel or crushed rock around it to hold it in place; top the gravel with colored rock. Place in a cool, shady spot.

To dry lavender, just clip the stems when blossoms are fully colored and hang them upside down. For best results with hydrangeas, however, don't pick the flower heads when their color is at its richest; wait until they have begun to fade and at least half the blossoms have turned greenish. Place the cut stems in a container holding an inch of water. The flowers will start to dry as the water evaporates; when it's gone, hang them upside down to finish drying.

MATERIALS & TOOLS 3 bunches green curly willow branches • 1 wire ring, 14 inches in diameter • Several stems hydrangea • Several stems statice • Several stems sea holly • Several snippets dusty miller foliage • Clippers

A Proper Path
and Sun-Shade Garden

A WELL-TRODDEN SHORTCUT from the driveway to the front door was a bit of an eyesore until the owners decided to turn it into an asset. The driveway's brick trim suggested the tidy edging for the new walkway, but since this is an informal approach, gravel and stepping-stones seemed appropriate for the path itself. The irregularly shaped flagstones were carefully chosen and positioned to accommodate the different strides of the 5-foot, 3-inch gardener and her husband, who stands a foot taller. Tidy clumps of agapanthus, sage, and bacopa—positioned so that each receives the amount of light or shade it requires—make up their own little garden under the birch tree.

BEFORE

ABOVE: **The owners were in the habit of cutting through the garden on their way to the front door. To give the rough but well-established path official standing, they added a brick border and flagstone pavers.**

Installing a Gravel Path with Brick Border

1 Before building the forms for the border, excavate the path area (plus 6 inches on either side to provide working space) to a depth of 4 inches. (In areas where the soil freezes, you may need to excavate deeper and add a layer of gravel to help prevent frost heaving; consult your local building department for advice.) Tamp the soil to make it firm and level.

Construct the forms from 2 by 4 lumber; hold forms in place with 1 by 2 stakes along the outside edges and check level often as you work. Place rebar down the middle of the forms; the wires embedded in dobies—small blocks of precast concrete—hold the rebar in place. Mix the concrete and shovel it into the forms.

2 Screed (level) the concrete by moving a board along the tops of the forms with a sawing motion. When the concrete is set, remove the forms. To cure the concrete, keep it damp for 3 to 7 days by covering it with plastic sheeting or sprinkling it frequently.

MATERIALS & TOOLS 2 by 4 lumber • 1 by 2 stakes, 1 foot long • Rebar • Dobies • Concrete mix • Mortar mix • Bricks • Coarse or builder's sand • Flagstones (1 to 2 inches thick) • Plastic sheeting • Landscape fabric • Gravel • Small sledgehammer • Tamper • Carpenter's level • 1 by 4 screed board (1 foot or more longer than width of brick border) • String (mason's line) • Brick trowel • Brick set • Safety glasses

Cutting a Brick

To cut a brick to size, use a brick set to score a line on all four sides. Make the cut with a sharp blow of a small sledgehammer on the brick set. Wear safety glasses.

3 To aid in alignment, run a string (mason's line) along the outside edge of the concrete border at the height of one brick; also use a carpenter's level often as you lay the bricks. Wet bricks so they won't suck moisture from the mortar. Mix mortar and spread a ½-inch-thick layer over concrete, enough to lay 3 or 4 bricks. Set the first brick in place on mortar. "Butter" end of next brick with mortar and join it to the first brick; the mortar joint should be about ½ inch thick. Continue in this way until border is complete.

4 Lay landscape fabric over the path between the borders. Spread 2 inches of dampened sand on the fabric. Tamp the sand to make it level and firm, sprinkling it lightly with water as you work.

5 Add about ½ inch more sand to accept the flagstones (don't tamp it down). Set flagstones in sand; they should be ½ to ¾ inch higher than the finished path (the added height helps keep gravel off the stones). If necessary, add or remove sand to adjust the height of the flagstones. Spread gravel over path and rake it smoothly around stones.

BELOW: **Fragrant chamomile and thyme grow between stepping-stones of a new gardener's path.**

A Secret Retreat

A PRIVATE GARDEN just inside the lattice that screens the front door never really achieved its potential when it also served as a pathway to a potting bench tucked into the side yard. After laying a new path around the other side of the screen for front garden access and to divert traffic to and from the potting area, the gardener turned this 7- by 10-foot corner into a private patio, furnished with a fancy wrought-iron bench and sturdy shelves for her orchid collection. Where there was bare dirt, the new garden now has a gravel surface. Large stepping-stones are set in the gravel, subtly repeating the use of these materials in other paths.

A bed of struggling plants at the entrance to the garden was replanted with ferns and coral bells. Japanese blood grass rises like a fountain from a large glazed urn set among leafy perennials. Next to the bed, ferns in pots extend the greenery into the patio and enhance the feeling of seclusion. Right beside the bench, a water garden in a pot makes a little splash of its own.

A Pond in a Pot

WATER GARDENS draw sparkling light down among the greenery and bring new plants to the gardener's repertoire. No garden is too small for a water feature in a pot.

This bright red ceramic pot was raised on an iron stand to put it literally at the fingertips of anyone sitting on the bench beside it. Curly tendrils of corkscrew rush stretch out playfully over the edge of the pot; a floating cluster of water hyacinths nestles alongside. Japanese blood grass and colorful Joseph's coat, which both adapt gracefully to the water, give the arrangement height.

TIP

FLOATING MOSQUITO-CONTROL RINGS CONTAIN A NATURALLY OCCURRING BACTERIUM THAT KILLS MOSQUITO LARVAE. TO TREAT A SMALL WATER FEATURE, BREAK UP A RING AND JUST USE A QUARTER OF IT.

Planting a Container Water Garden

1 Select a glazed container with no drainage hole. Transplant rooted plants to terra-cotta or plastic pots, using ordinary garden topsoil. (Packaged potting mix tends to be too light and floats into the water.) Spread a ½-inch-deep layer of pebbles atop soil in each pot to keep it in place. Bring plants to the correct height by setting the pots on other pots or on a brick.

2 Arrange the potted plants in the container, setting the taller ones to the side or at the back.

3 Before filling the container with water, move it to its permanent position—once filled, it will be very heavy. Check that the container is level, then finish adding water. Add a mosquito-control ring and tuck in any floating plants. Add water as needed to keep the container full. (To help keep water clean, periodically overfill the container, so that some of the old water flows out, taking dead leaves and debris with it.)

BELOW: **This water garden features corkscrew rush, Japanese blood grass, red-leafed Joseph's coat, and floating water hyacinth. Periodically thin or cut back plants that outgrow their allotted space.**

MATERIALS Large glazed ceramic container • Aquatic and moisture-loving plants • Small terra-cotta or plastic pots • Topsoil • Pebbles • Bricks (optional) • Mosquito-control ring

A Collector's Abundant Welcome

A CAREFULLY CHOREOGRAPHED arrangement of plants in pots transformed a severe entryway into a cheerful, colorful garden framing the stairs. Lovely cymbidium orchids are the standouts of this shade-tolerant grouping.

BEFORE

There was room on the landing for a couple of large plants, but otherwise the steps were kept clear. The other pots are arranged so the plants seem to ascend with the stairs; the line of pots at right opens out in a welcoming gesture.

The gardener grows his potted orchids in a slightly sunnier location until their long bloom period begins, then moves them here. He places them on upside-down flower pots, if necessary, to bring them up to the rim of a cachepot. The other plants are handsome in their glazed pots and can remain beside the stairs all year.

CHALLENGE

The all-concrete entryway was stark and inhospitable. Not even a small strip of soil was available for plantings.

Blooming plants were needed to brighten the welcome, but heavy shade limited the choices.

SOLUTION

Colorful pots filled with bright orchids and lush foliage transform the entry into an inviting welcome.

Cymbidium orchids grow in a sunny spot until blossom time, then move here—where they bloom happily in the shady entry.

PLANT HIGHLIGHTS

Chamaedorea seifrizii

Cymbidium hybrids

Lily-of-the-valley shrub
Pieris japonica

Ternstroemia gymnanthera

On the Right Path

THIS FRONT YARD garden gave visitors mixed messages: the path from the street, made with widely spaced squares of bricks set in gravel, was little more than a suggestion, and it met the concrete front walk in an awkward way. To welcome guests properly and bring the yard together, the owners replaced the brick pads and a side concrete path with new walks made of wide flagstone slabs.

BEFORE

A haphazard mix of shrubs and grasses on one side of the path was replaced with a richly textured garden of ground cover plants under the canopy of a Japanese maple. On the opposite side, the owners built the soil up into a berm, where they planted and spotlighted a specimen weeping Japanese maple. The same tapestry of ornamental grasses, baby's tears, and other low-growing plants flow around the base of the maple.

Rugged, in-scale boulders on either side give the walk the look of a placid stream flowing through a natural landscape.

PLANT HIGHLIGHTS

Fern pine
Podocarpus gracilior

Hen and chicks
Echeveria hybrids

Hosta

Japanese aucuba (variegated)
Aucuba japonica

Japanese forest grass
Hakonechloa macra 'Aurea'

Japanese maples
Acer palmatum varieties

CHALLENGE

The shady yard was uninteresting and flat; plantings were poorly chosen.

Widely spaced brick pads forced visitors to take giant steps or walk on bare soil; the path was narrow and dark.

SOLUTION

Japanese maples and an eye-catching berm planted with low-growing plants create an inviting garden.

A wide, smooth flagstone path and warm path lighting welcome visitors to the front door.

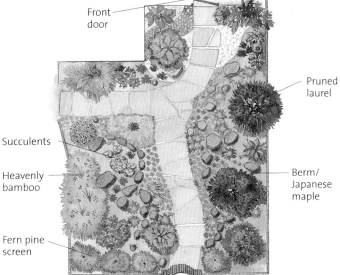

Front door

Pruned laurel

Succulents

Heavenly bamboo

Berm/ Japanese maple

Fern pine screen

Lighting the Way

PROPER LIGHTING makes a walkway easy to navigate after dark, and a well-lit path also highlights the plantings around it. Decorative fixtures from a builder's supply store or a lighting shop can be chosen to complement the garden's style without stealing the show.

The owners of this garden replaced the existing fixtures with stylish copper lamps on either side of a new flagstone path. Whether the lights are placed on one or both sides of a walk, they should be spaced so their beams overlap slightly, illuminating the area evenly. The fixtures themselves should be set back just far enough to be out of the way when you sweep the walk, but close enough to it to allow the light to reach most of the way across.

TIP

A LOW-VOLTAGE OUTDOOR LIGHTING SYSTEM, WHICH USES A TRANSFORMER TO REDUCE REGULAR HOUSEHOLD CURRENT TO 12 VOLTS, IS SAFE AND EASY TO INSTALL. LOOK FOR A SYSTEM KIT WITH A TIMER AND ON-OFF SWITCH.

Cutting Flagstone

If you need to cut flagstones, use a sharp tool such as a brick set to score a ⅛-inch-deep groove across the stone. Place a length of lumber under the stone so the part to be removed and the scored line overhang it. Make the cut by striking sharply on the brick set with a hammer or small sledgehammer. Wear safety glasses.

Laying a Flagstone Path

1 Mark the edges of the path with string and stakes.

2 Dig out the soil to a depth of 4 inches. If you like, you can use the excavated soil to make a berm. Tamp the soil to make it firm; check depth again. Then spread 2 inches of base rock or crushed gravel over soil. Tamp again, leveling the gravel.

3 Spread about 1 inch of sand over the path to accept the flagstones (don't tamp it down). The flagstones should be about ½ inch above ground level after they're set in place.

4 Set flagstones on sand, moving them around until you find a pleasing arrangement that requires a minimum of cutting. Settle each stone in place by tapping it several times with a rubber mallet. Use a carpenter's level placed on a long board to check that the path is level. Add or remove sand as needed to make path level and adjust height of stones. Finally, sweep dampened sand into the cracks.

MATERIALS & TOOLS Base rock or crushed gravel • Coarse or builder's sand • Flagstones, 1 to 2 inches thick • Stakes, 1 foot long • Hammer or small sledgehammer • Rubber mallet • Tamper • Carpenter's level • String (mason's line) • Brick set • Safety glasses

Installing Low-voltage Path Lighting

1 Plan the general layout of the path lighting. Where the cable must go under a path, feed it through a length of PVC pipe (a chase pipe). This will save you having to disturb the path if you need to move the lighting in the future. To snip cables, use wire cutters; reconnect cables with weatherproof wire connectors. Bury the pipe in a trench about 6 inches deep.

2 Though cable for low-voltage lighting can be laid on the surface of the ground (concealed by mulch), it's safer to bury it in a trench so you won't trip on it. The protection of PVC pipe is needed only under paths.

3 Set the light fixtures in place. Follow the kit directions to connect them to the cable. Mentally note where the cables are (or mark their location physically) so you won't accidentally slice them when digging in the garden.

MATERIALS & TOOLS Low-voltage outdoor lighting system (kits sold at building supply stores) • PVC pipe, 1½ inches in diameter • Wire cutters • Weatherproof wire connectors

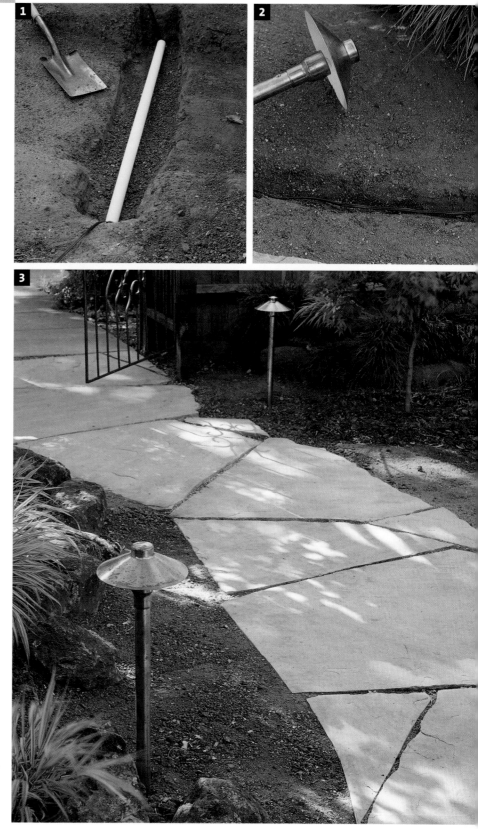

New Life for an Old Shrub

TIP

PRUNING CAN BE INTIMIDATING. YOU ARE, AFTER ALL, MEDDLING WITH NATURE. JUST REMEMBER, A GARDEN IS A COLLABORATION WITH NATURE. REMOVE DEAD BRANCHES, THOSE THAT CROSS EACH OTHER, AND ANY THAT BLOCK YOUR WAY OR GROW TOO CLOSE TO THE HOUSE. WHEN A TREE OR SHRUB IS BADLY OVER-GROWN OR HAS BEEN CLIPPED INTO AN UNFLATTERING FORM, CAREFUL PRUNING BRINGS OUT THE ARCHITECTURE OF THE LIMBS AND LETS LIGHT AND AIR INTO THE PLANT. ALWAYS USE SHARP TOOLS. A GOOD PAIR OF LOPPERS AND A SMALL TREE SAW SHOULD BE ALL YOU NEED.

MATURE SHRUBS are an asset in any garden, but when a shrub starts to overwhelm the landscape, crowding paths and stealing light from the plants around it, you

BEFORE

may need to prune it to bring the garden back into balance.

This English laurel was healthy, but it had become oppressively dense. Professional arborists removed about one-third of the branches, raising the canopy and giving it a more natural shape. Good pruning isn't based on a formula: you have to study the plant's natural shape and interpret it, making one cut at a time. Use a pole saw to reach branches above your head. If the work requires climbing into the tree with a chain saw, it's best to call an expert.

DO IT TODAY

Marvelous Maples

FEW TREES CAN MATCH the beauty and character of Japanese maples, which have been grown in Japan for more than 300 years. There are hundreds of varieties, suitable for gardens large and small as well as for containers. The red-leafed variety shown here is planted on a berm that raises the soil grade about 2½ feet above the front walk. The shallow-rooted tree will thrive with the excellent drainage the berm provides, and its placement at the top of the mound, among tufts of Japanese forest grass, hostas, and baby's tears, allows an especially good view of its delicate branches and weeping habit.

TIP

SEVERAL DAYS BEFORE MOVING THE TREE, SOAK THE SOIL AROUND IT. MOIST SOIL HELPS THE ROOT BALL HOLD TOGETHER, AND A WELL-WATERED PLANT ALSO SUFFERS LESS STRESS WHEN MOVED.

Transplanting a Small Tree

1 Mark a digging line in the soil around the tree, making it about one-third of the tree's height away from the trunk. If space allows, dig an 8-inch-wide trench just beyond this line to give yourself more working room. Work your way under the root ball, severing roots that extend into the trench. Once the root ball has been freed, work a piece of burlap or heavy plastic under and around it; then wrap securely. The burlap holds the root ball together and prevents the roots from drying out. Lift the tree by holding the root ball, not the trunk (which could pull away from the roots).

2 Dig a new hole for the tree; it should be the same depth as the root ball and a foot or so wider. Rough up the sides and bottom

Gardening at a Higher Level

When the owners dug a level bed for the new path, they transferred the excavated soil to one side of the garden, creating a low mound—a berm. Berms increase available planting area and showcase specimen plants. At the front of a property, a well-planted berm provides privacy, partially screening the garden from the street.

with a spading fork or the edge of a shovel to help the roots penetrate the soil. Place the tree in the hole and remove the burlap.

3 Lay a tool handle or stake across the hole to check that top of root ball is at the original level. If the tree is planted too deep, the trunk may rot; if it's set too high, the roots may dry out. Add or remove soil to bring tree to correct depth. Fill the hole with excavated soil. Water well, soaking root ball and surrounding soil. Spread a 2- to 3-inch layer of mulch (such as ground bark) around the tree, taking care not to pile it against the trunk.

MATERIALS & TOOLS Burlap or heavy plastic sheeting • Stake or tool handle • Mulch

Harmonious Blend

IDEAS BORROWED FROM Japanese garden design helped create a serene mood around this front door. An unsightly downspout was replaced with a traditional Japanese rain chain, which falls onto a bed of pebbles. Stones and water are essential elements of Asian gardens; here, the smooth-surfaced stones create the illusion of a small creekbed. When it rains, water cascades down the chain, splashes quietly onto the pebbles, and drains away.

BEFORE

28

TIP

BESIDES THE CLASSIC RAIN

CHAIN SHOWN HERE, A MODEL

IS AVAILABLE FEATURING

A STRING OF COPPER CUPS;

AS RAIN RUSHES FROM THE

GUTTER, IT CASCADES THROUGH

THE CUPS. IF YOUR DOWN-

SPOUTS ARE EXTRA LONG,

YOU CAN PURCHASE A 3-FOOT

EXTENSION FOR THE RAIN

CHAIN OR COPPER RAIN CUPS.

Installing a Rain Chain

1 If necessary, clean debris and leaves from the gutter. Detach the downspout's brackets from the wall. Standing on a ladder, detach the downspout from the gutter. You will see a ring around the drain hole that leads from the gutter to the downspout; leave this ring in place.

2 Straighten out the wire at the top of the rain chain to make a U-shape. A decorative copper ring is provided with the kit; place it over the wire so that it rests on the first link of the rain chain. Slip the wire up through the drain hole into the gutter; cross the ends of the wire over each other and bend them down on either side along the gut-ter to hold the rain chain firmly in place. The decorative copper ring should rest just below the drain hole, camouflaging it.

3 If desired, excavate a shallow hole and position a concrete or plastic splash block under the end of the rain chain, with its open end pointed away from the house. Conceal the splash block with decorative stones, so that the chain appears to disappear into a low mound of stones.

MATERIALS & TOOLS Rain chain kit • Ladder • Concrete or plastic splash block (optional) • Decorative stones (optional)

The Elements of Style

A WELL-DESIGNED garden always makes a pretty picture, but when you take a closer look, the details should be just as eloquent as the whole. A thoughtful combination of materials, plants, and ornaments is essential to a successful design: keep the entire garden in mind as you select and place each of the details.

This gardener enjoys the color and character of succulent plants, but succulents are not really suited to shady gardens like hers. Still, she sought out the sunniest spot, and then made room there for a small, spreading clump of hen and chicks.

Large rocks were used throughout to evoke natural landscapes. The lichen-encrusted stones sparkle like huge jewels among the foliage plants growing on a gentle berm. The stones help hold the soil in place and create a cool environment for the plants' roots.

Texture, color, and shape all work together to express serenity in a Japanese garden. A simple terra-cotta urn, tucked among the gold-spotted leaves of aucuba and the spiky foliage of lily turf, glows serenely in a quiet corner, seeming almost to radiate the warmth of the sun.

ABOVE: **Sun splashes on the blue-green rosettes of hen and chicks.**
RIGHT: **Labrador violets, lily turf, and Japanese forest grass nestle against a lichen-spotted stone.**
BELOW: **A terra-cotta urn catches the light in front of a decorative ironwork panel.**

A Living Screen

IF YOU LIVE on a busy street, traffic noise invades the privacy of your garden. It's impossible to make it go away, but a tall screen of evergreens will soften the noise and keep the cars out of sight. The plant you choose for a hedge should be hardy, disease resistant, and fairly thick foliaged; it should look good throughout the year and thrive with little attention.

The owners of this garden planted fern pines just inside their privacy fence. The line of slim, upright evergreens will eventually grow together into a tall, attractive hedge that will significantly muffle the sound of cars passing by just outside the gate.

BEFORE

31

Eastern Influence, Western Exposure

THE POSSIBILITIES of this tiny front yard were stifled by overgrown shrubs that obscured the front windows, narrowed the entryway, and hid the architectural play between the house and the garage. Once the domineering shrubs came out, there was plenty of room for a stylish Asian garden that re-

BEFORE

defines the relationship between house, garden, and street.

A low fence now frames the garden, separating the private yard from the sidewalk. A simple pergola over the entryway and front windows brings the garden right up to the house without blocking the light.

The front lawn was removed and replaced with low-maintenance plants, set among weathered stones in low berms along the course of a dry streambed. A fieldstone path follows the dry stream across the garden, then branches off around the side of the house.

PLANT HIGHLIGHTS

Chinese wisteria
Wisteria sinensis

Fortnight lily
Dietes iridioides

Heavenly bamboo
Nandina domestica

Japanese maple
Acer palmatum

Mugho pine
Pinus mugo mugo

Western sword fern
Polystichum munitum

CHALLENGE

Drab plantings accentuated the plain, unappealing front yard.

The overgrown shrubs darkened and narrowed the entryway.

SOLUTION

Asian-style garden now features planted berms, dry streambed, stone sculpture, and stepping-stone path.

Two-level pergola complements the architecture and the garden style.

Gateway Welcome

THE FRONT GATE'S gleaming cedar panels and subtle bamboo ornament harmonize with the garden's Asian theme. Container-grown plants make a soft, leafy frame for the gate and dramatize the architecture of the entranceway. The striking black-glazed pot was chosen especially for the variegated Japanese maple, a dwarf variety that grows to only 7 feet tall.

Just beside the gate, the gardener placed a rough granite water basin whose color and texture complement the natural materials in the garden. A clump of lily turf makes a quiet splash beside the basin.

IN INFORMAL GARDENS,
CONTAINERS PLANTED WITH
GRACEFUL BAMBOO OR
ORNAMENTAL GRASSES WILL
HIDE A UTILITY METER, AN
AIR-CONDITIONING UNIT, OR
TRASH BINS. IN MORE FORMAL
SETTINGS, BOXWOOD, YEWS,
AND OTHER EVERGREENS
WORK NICELY.

ABOVE: **Japanese maples are
decorative and adaptable, and
many are well known for their
brilliant leaf color. Gardeners
love them for the infinite variety
of their foliage, such as the lacy
leaves of the *Acer palmatum*
'Dissectum' shown here.**

Green Screen of Container Plantings

TRASH AND RECYCLING BINS are kept out of sight behind a group of three good-sized glazed pots, each holding an exuberant specimen plant. A large pot of bamboo is enough to hide the bins. Contrasting plantings in pots of different sizes give depth and variety to an almost sculptural arrangement that's set off by the handsome brick paving. The low bowl contains variegated Japanese sweet flag, a water-loving plant; in the middle is fortnight lily, which thrives in large containers. This deceptively simple arrangement creates a lively and sophisticated landscape in miniature, like a little echo of the rest of the garden here at the corner of the garage.

A Gardener's Pot Luck

A BRICK PLANTER was all the acreage this avid gardener had to work with when he moved into his condominium. He turned the 4- by 12-foot planter into a sophisticated rock garden and put the entry area to work as a showcase for more than a dozen plants in pots.

BEFORE

Browsing deer are a constant threat to the plant collection, but New Zealand flax, a long-blooming hardy geranium, and fragrant thyme, oregano, and lavender have proved to be mostly deerproof. A striking variegated century plant, well armed with sharp spines, stands guard by the planter.

The garden welcomes guests to the door and provides a cheerful view from the living room windows, too. Glazed and unglazed pots of various shapes and sizes contribute to the overall exuberance of the scene.

CHALLENGE

A drab façade, an aggregate walk, and a single, almost barren planter created an unappealing entry.

The front walk is also a deer trail, so any plantings are fair game for these garden marauders.

SOLUTION

A rock garden in the planter and a bright selection of plants in pots extend a cheery welcome.

The thoughtful selection of deer-resistant plants helps ensure the garden's success.

PLANT HIGHLIGHTS

African daisy
Osteospermum fruticosum

Century plant
Agave americana 'Striata'

English lavender
Lavandula angustifolia

New Zealand flax
Phormium tenax hybrids

Oregano
Origanum 'Kent Beauty'

Thrift
Armeria

Waterwise Oasis

THE OWNERS OF THIS LOW-SLUNG ranch house broke with tradition and eliminated the Bermuda grass lawn around their home. They replaced it with a dazzling low-maintenance garden tough enough to take the heat. Their corner lot gave them plenty of room to work with.

The new garden, defined by wide, gentle berms  that run along either side of the flagstone front walk, combines fast-growing annuals with tough, drought-tolerant perennials, ornamental grasses, and small trees. Great drifts of bright annual poppies among the other plants knit the garden together. Poppies, toadflax, gaillardias, and an occasional thistle also help hold the silty clay soil in place while the permanent plantings are becoming established. Butterflies and humming-birds are regular visitors.

In fall, clumps of pink muhly grass are covered with feathery flower plumes, spreading a dramatic purplish pink mist over the garden.

BEFORE

PLANT HIGHLIGHTS

Anacacho orchid tree
Bauhinia lunarioides

California poppy
Eschscholzia californica

Gaillardia

Mesquite
Prosopis

Pink muhly
Muhlenbergia capillaris

Flanders field poppy
Papaver rhoeas

CHALLENGE

Owners no longer wanted a water-demanding lawn.

New permanent plantings were slow to establish; garden looked bare.

SOLUTION

Low-maintenance, drought-tolerant plants replace the lawn.

Quick-growing annuals and other plants fill the garden while slower-to-establish plants mature.

From Plain to Fancy

A NEW FRONT WALK and a lush garden alongside it changed the character of this ranch house from solemn to smart. In the process of updating their entryway, the homeowners also redesigned the driveway, creating a generous parking area as well as adding a raised bed with dry-stacked stones.

BEFORE

Trailing plants spill from the raised bed, softening the edge of the drive.

The original walk ran across the yard parallel to the house, cutting like a ravine from the driveway to the front door. The new stone walkway leads directly up from the parking area, opening up the approach to the house. Shade-loving plants thrive in the dappled light under a mature oak tree along the walk. Plants in pots on the front steps take the garden right to the door.

A single substantial column supports the eaves over the stoop. The dark green door offers a finishing, welcoming touch.

PLANT HIGHLIGHTS

Fancy-leafed caladium
Caladium bicolor

Impatiens

Maiden grass
Miscanthus sinensis 'Gracillimus'

Southern magnolia
Magnolia grandiflora 'Little Gem'

Southern shield fern
Thelypteris kunthii

Wishbone flower
Torenia fournieri

40

CHALLENGE

Long, narrow driveway made parking and backing out difficult.

The front walk, sunken and laid close to the house wall, didn't enhance the home's entryway.

SOLUTION

Redesigned garden and drive offer ample parking and an inviting entry.

New walk gently curves directly to door; pretty landscaping and potted plants add to the welcome.

A Blaze of
Color

Flashy and Fearless

Dramatic colors and contrasts set Southwestern gardens
apart. Here, a hawthorn tree flashes shimmering gold fall
foliage against pink adobe walls and a sparkling blue door
accented with decorative iron hardware and a wreath of

Whimsical Welcome

BELOW: An arbored gate at the end of a garden path is actually just for show. The owners painted an old gate red and hung it between two fence posts to make an instant focal point.

Blue Mood

ABOVE: If the garden doesn't have a view, you can always paint one to suit. This strictly imaginary hillside landscape creates a dreamy background for a comfortable seating area.

Garden Window

BELOW: Ruby red trim brings a window in a pale stucco wall to life. An airy, living valance of wisteria, with its clusters of purple and white blooms, adds depth—and romance—to the setting.

Divide and Multiply

Dramatically painted concrete walls, one of them centered with shimmering glass blocks, define areas in this small garden and provide privacy. The sunny Caribbean colors create lively outdoor rooms.

Heavenly View

RIGHT: The pale trunk and branches of an espaliered pomegranate stretch up and across a deep red courtyard wall. The limbs are carefully pruned to frame a simple niche, from which a terra-cotta saint watches over the garden.

Bouquet Olé!

BELOW: Annual and perennial flowers in dazzling variety seem to explode from a clay pot guarded by a vigilant folk-art dog. Behind the pot, stucco walls flame in sunset colors. Silvery foliage adds sparkle to the arrangement.

Burning Bright

BELOW: The warm red walls around this outdoor fireplace make a dramatic backdrop for bold accessories. Here, a richly patterned glazed platter hangs above the mantle; a pair of standard-trained rosemary plants in vivid pots decorates a high chimney shelf.

Purple Craze

ABOVE: **A bold mix of foliage textures and shapes and hot flower colors reveals the hand of an adventurous gardener. The fearless palette extends all the way to the back door, which is painted a daring paint-box purple.**

Garden to Go

LEFT: **An old wheelbarrow with a fresh coat of blue paint and a full load of foxgloves steals the show from the flower bed in the background. The wheelbarrow can be moved to suit the gardener's fancy.**

Sapphire Sculpture

These old camellia trunks have been pruned and painted blue to accent their sculptural form. Deep pink flower petals fall to the ground, contrasting handsomely with the sleek surfaces of stem and stone.

Natural Connections

A TYPICAL SIDE YARD may not be much wider than a wheel-barrow with a wide load, but don't be discouraged by the narrow space. There's often just enough room for a garden.

Plain concrete pavers streaked like a runway through this side yard, bleakly discouraging development of the area on either side. A new line of slate stepping-stones slowed things down and began the transformation of the setting into a pretty garden. Fragrant angel's trumpet flourishes in the shady, sheltered area. In summer, the owner moves her orchids here where they thrive with ferns in the understory. To open up the space, a makeshift potting area against the fence was moved to a new space. Hanging baskets now provide color without crowding the narrow garden.

CHALLENGE

Heavy shade and a straight path of concrete pavers seemed to make the cramped side yard even narrower.

A single shelf on the fence was all the gardener had for a potting area.

SOLUTION

A meandering path and leafy, shade-loving plants give the garden a wider feel and a lush, tropical air.

A new potting area, complete with bench and storage, provides a pleasant place to work.

BEFORE

In gardening, whether we know it or not, we are in a world of connections.…Even a small garden owes much to far-flung places.

—ALLEN LACY
The Inviting Garden

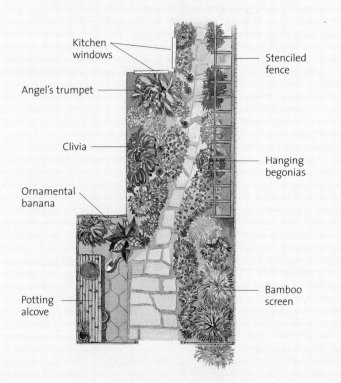

Kitchen windows

Angel's trumpet

Clivia

Ornamental banana

Potting alcove

Stenciled fence

Hanging begonias

Bamboo screen

Potting Alcove

EVERY GARDENER needs a place to keep tools and potting soil. This gardener tried hiding a plastic storage unit on the side of his house, but it wasn't attractive, so he decided to remove it.

Next, he paved the area with concrete stepping-stones recycled from an old path, then acid-stained. The new alcove is walled with bamboo panels, which serve as a pegboard for tools; a heavier panel, supported by large bamboo posts, makes a fine potting bench.

BEFORE

50

Acid-staining Concrete Stepping-stones

1 To make the potting alcove floor shown here, consider reusing old concrete pavers, if possible. Set them close together on raked and leveled soil. Place a small amount of sand under the pavers to help stabilize and level them. Then, acid-stain.

Before staining, wash the pavers with concrete cleaner, rinse with water, and let dry thoroughly. To prevent chemicals from contaminating nearby areas, dig a narrow trench around the perimeter of the concrete to be stained; fill the trench with sand.

Wear all the safety gear listed below. Following label directions, pour a portion of the stain into an acid-resistant bucket. Dip an acid-resistant brush into the solution and scrub the stain onto the concrete in a figure-eight pattern; take care not to spatter stain. Work on small areas of concrete at a time, keeping the edges wet as you move to new areas. Store unused stain in the bucket.

2 After about 4 hours, wipe up the chemical residue with rags; place used rags in the second acid-resistant bucket. Rinse the concrete

with water and let it dry. Remove sand from the trench, placing it in the bucket with the rags.

3 Before sealing concrete to protect the surface, apply a neutralizing rinse solution, following label directions. After 5 minutes, mop up solution with clean rags, then place them in second bucket. Rinse with water; let dry for 72 hours. Seal concrete with a clear water-based sealer, following label directions. Dispose of buckets and their contents at your community's hazardous-waste disposal site.

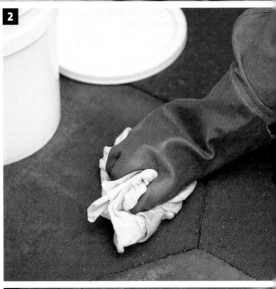

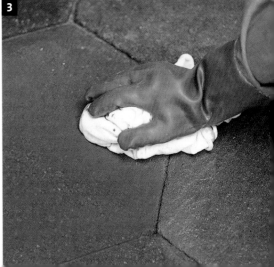

MATERIALS & TOOLS Sand • Concrete cleaner • Stain manufactured for concrete (acid-stain solution) • Neutralizing rinse solution • Clear water-based concrete sealer • 2 acid-resistant buckets with tight-fitting lids • Acid-resistant brush • Old clothing (stain does not wash out) • Rags • **Safety gear:** P100/hydrogen chloride respirator; goggles; chemical-resistant gloves, apron, and boots

Whimsical Stencils

BOLD FOLIAGE and bright flowers in the tropical garden outside the kitchen window brought lots of color inside, but the gardener thought the scene needed a fun and artful touch—so he painted a parade of jaunty green-and-yellow iguanas on the horizontal planks along the top of the fence. Iguanas aren't that easy to draw, but by using a stencil kit purchased from a mail-order supplier, you can get it right every time and create as many you want.

The whimsical lizards are just at eye level when you stand at the kitchen sink. They wouldn't really be native to this garden, but they still look right at home.

ABOVE: The new garden improves the view from an important spot: the kitchen sink. A lush tropical garden and playful iguanas replace the old view of an open storage shed.

TIP

FOR BEST RESULTS IN STENCIL-
ING, START WITH A DRY
BRUSH. DIP THE BRUSH IN THE
PAINT, THEN WIPE IT FIRMLY
ON A PAPER TOWEL. THIS
WORKS THE PAINT INTO THE
BRUSH WITHOUT OVERLOAD-
ING IT. TO APPLY PAINT, DAB IT
ONTO THE SURFACE RATHER
THAN STROKING IT ON.

Stenciling on Weathered Wood

1 Using overlay stencils, you can paint designs more complicated than those you can produce with single stencils (see page 61, "Refinishing a Wooden Bench," for a single-stencil project). Before using the stencils, practice first on paper, then on a scrap of the same kind of wood you plan to stencil.

To clean the weathered wood surface, lightly brush it with a soft whisk broom, taking care not to raise the grain or roughen the wood surface.

Arrange paints, a paper plate, and brushes on the ladder's paint tray. Squeeze small pools of paints onto plate. Tape the first overlay to the wood surface with masking tape. Mark through the registration holes onto the wood with a white-leaded pencil. The pencil marks will be used to align the stencil overlay.

2 Using one of the broader stencil brushes, dab on medium green paint to color the iguana's body; take care not to force paint under the edges of the stencil. Using a narrower brush, dab on golden yellow for the feet. Remove the first overlay.

3 Tape the second overlay to the surface, making sure its registration holes line up with the white marks. Using a medium-size brush and dark green paint, add body details and shadows. Remove the stencil.

Add finishing touches as desired. Here, the gardener painted yellow highlights on the iguana's body and stenciled a bright orange butterfly on the fence for it to chase.

MATERIALS & TOOLS Overlay iguana stencil • Dark green, medium green, and golden yellow paint for stencils, as noted in stencil instructions • Stencil brushes • White-leaded pencil • Soft-bristled whisk broom • Paper plate • Paper towels • Masking tape • Ladder with paint tray

Second Life for a Small Side Yard

AN UNDISTINGUISHED APPROACH to a side gate ran along a blank wall, with nothing to set it off from the neighbor's yard. To create an inviting passageway and define the edge of her property at the same time, the gardener installed an attractive bamboo fence. The style, as elsewhere in the garden, is Asian.

BEFORE

The fence is made from panels of split-bamboo screening mounted on a wooden frame. A path of heavy fieldstones, set in sand in a pattern reminiscent of a child's hopscotch game, gently guides the visitor to the gate. Lily turf and ferns, planted among large rocks, flourish with little attention in the dappled light on either side of the path. The smooth, handsome branches of a mature Japanese maple frame the approach.

CHALLENGE

Neglected space was open to the busy yard and recycling cans and bins next door.

Narrow, shaded area presented difficult growing conditions.

SOLUTION

New bamboo fencing is perfect scale for the small space; it buffers noise and provides privacy.

Shade lovers such as hellebores thrive in the new side yard. A stone path creates a pleasant transition from backyard to front.

A Fountain Becomes the Focus

BLOOMING AZALEAS brought a brief moment of colorful cheer to this side yard in spring, but for most of the year the space was dark and dour. The owner decided to freshen it up by replacing some of the old shrubs with a more interesting collection of plants and adding a fountain.

BEFORE

The shady garden had never really had a coherent design. Now, the spill fountain serves as the central feature, and the plantings seem to flow around it. The owner found the Asian jar at a garden shop and made the fountain herself.

The beds are about 10 feet wide, easily providing enough room to layer the plantings. Ferns, hellebores, hydrangeas, and an exotic-looking Japanese aralia all thrive in the filtered sunlight. The cool green retreat offers a peaceful respite from the busy world outside.

PLANT HIGHLIGHTS

Foamflower
Tiarella 'Iron Butterfly'

Hellebore
Helleborus × hybridus

Japanese aralia
Fatsia japonica

Maidenhair fern
Adiantum raddianum

Vine maple
Acer circinatum

CHALLENGE

Narrow, dark corridor looked gloomy; the shady exposure created a difficult growing environment.

The garden had no unifying theme.

SOLUTION

New garden design makes the yard look wider; a bright red bench offers a resting place to ponder the view.

A glossy earth-toned fountain creates an attractive focal point and connects the elements of the garden.

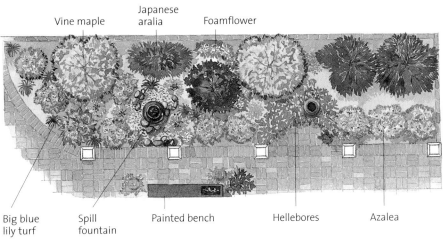

Vine maple   Japanese aralia   Foamflower

Big blue lily turf   Spill fountain   Painted bench   Hellebores   Azalea

Spill Fountain

THE QUIET SPLASHING of a spill fountain unobtrusively changes the mood of the garden—and of the gardener. A small fountain hidden in an elegant ceramic urn brings a lively play of light and shadow to a corner of the garden. A bright pot sparkles even more richly when a trickle of water glazes its sides and reflected sunlight flashes at its brim.

Spill fountains are best used as accents. Choose a sculptural pot and place it somewhere along a garden path or close to the porch or patio, where you can hear the trickling water and enjoy the reflections as you come and go.

TIP

IF YOU'RE PLANNING TO
LOCATE YOUR SPILL FOUNTAIN
MORE THAN A FEW FEET AWAY
FROM THE POWER SOURCE
FOR THE PUMP, PROTECT THE
PUMP'S CORD BY PUSHING
IT THROUGH A CONDUIT.

Creating a Spill Fountain

1 Dig a hole as deep as and 2 inches wider than the plastic tub. Center the tub in the hole and check that the rim is level. To help support the sides, backfill the hole with some of the excavated soil. Tamp down the soil and check again for level; adjust the tub if necessary.

2 With a masonry bit, drill a hole for the vinyl tubing in one side of the cinder block. Place the block in the plastic tub (the block will support the weight of the pot). Slide one end of the vinyl tubing over the fountain spout of the pump; snake the other end through the hole in the cinder block toward the center of the plastic tub. Lead the pump cord out of the tub and toward a grounded power source.

3 Cut a piece of heavy-gauge wire mesh at least 6 inches wider than the plastic tub; then lay it over the tub. Using tin snips, cut a hole in the center of the mesh, making it wide enough for the vinyl tubing to pass through easily. Bend the cut edges of mesh back so they do not damage the tubing.

4 Lower the pot onto the mesh, centering it on the cinder block. As you lower the pot, pull the tubing through the pot's drainage hole; it should reach halfway up the interior of the pot. Make sure the pot is level. Spread silicone sealant around the drainage hole and tubing and let it cure. Fill the pot and the tub below it with water and plug in the pump. Spread pebbles over the wire mesh, placing most of the larger pebbles toward the edges; trim off any excess mesh.

MATERIALS & TOOLS Ceramic pot with drainage hole • Plastic tub (at least a few inches deeper than pump is tall and 3 inches wider than the ceramic pot) • Cinder block (about as tall as plastic tub is deep; use two blocks if necessary) • Small submersible pump • Vinyl tubing (sized to fit fountain spout of pump and long enough to reach halfway up inside of ceramic pot) • Heavy-gauge wire mesh • Silicone sealant • Electric drill and masonry bit • Conduit (optional) • Pebbles • Carpenter's level • Tin snips

A Painted Bench

A FEW COATS OF PAINT and a stylish stencil turned an ordinary garage-sale bench into a thing of beauty. The glossy red paint, like fine Chinese lacquer, and the delicate stenciled tracery of pine needles and pinecones complement the Asian theme of the small garden.

The bench is centered under a bedroom window, facing a fountain. Plants in pots around the bench connect it to the rest of the garden: the big leaves of Japanese aralia and the foliage of five-finger fern are also to be found in the bed on the other side of the brick walk.

TIP

THE COLORS USED FOR THIS BENCH—DEEP RED, PURE BLACK, AND SOFTLY CONTRASTING GREEN—GIVE IT A DISTINCTLY ORIENTAL APPEARANCE.

60

Refinishing a Bench

1 Clean and sand the bench, if necessary. Use a drop cloth or newspapers to protect nearby surfaces. Apply three light coats of red satin spray paint, covering all parts of the bench. Let the paint dry between coats as directed on the can.

2 Make a background for the stencil by noting the outside measurements of the stencil form. Mark this area, which will be painted black, on the bench. Protect the surrounding area of the bench from the black paint with painter's masking tape (it won't pull off existing paint when removed) and newspaper. Apply the paint; let dry completely. Remove the tape and newspaper.

3 Tape the stencil form in place with painter's masking tape on the black rectangle. Dab on sage green paint in the cut-out areas, using a stencil brush; take care not to force paint under the edges of the stencil. (For more on stenciling, see "Stenciling on Weathered Wood," page 53.)

4 Remove the stencil and let the paint dry for 24 hours. Brush on a coat of satin polyurethane to protect the bench finish.

MATERIALS & TOOLS 1 wooden bench, 6 feet long • 2 or 3 cans red satin spray enamel • 1 can black satin spray enamel • 1 bottle sage green enamel for stencil • 1 pint satin polyurethane • Pinecone branch stencil • Stencil brush • Paintbrush • Painter's masking tape • Drop cloth or newspapers

Recycling Just Got Neater

IT'S EASY TO CLOSE the back door and pretend that the jumble of trash, recycling bins, and garbage cans outside doesn't exist—but that only works while you're in the house. When you're out in the garden, you don't want to look at trash cans. Building an attractive storage shelter large enough to hold everything solves the problem.

This conveniently located recycling center, which was designed and painted to look like it has always been part of the house, took two weekends to build. Before, newspapers piled up in the laundry room indoors so they wouldn't get soaked by rain. Now they are kept in their own bin, safely out of the weather. Trash cans, recyclables, and garden supplies, once crowded together under the narrow eaves, are all tucked neatly out of sight in the new shelter.

CHALLENGE

The side yard was an eyesore—a muddle of trash cans, recycling bins, and containers.

Newspapers had to be kept indoors until recycling day, to protect them from the weather.

SOLUTION

A handsome recycle center houses trash cans and recyclable bottles and cans.

Newspapers are safely tucked away in their own bin inside the shelter.

BEFORE

TIP

PLANT A COUPLE OF EASY-TO-CARE-FOR, COMPACT EVERGREENS AT EITHER END OF THE STRUCTURE TO HELP IT BLEND IN WITH THE SURROUNDINGS.

Recycle Shop

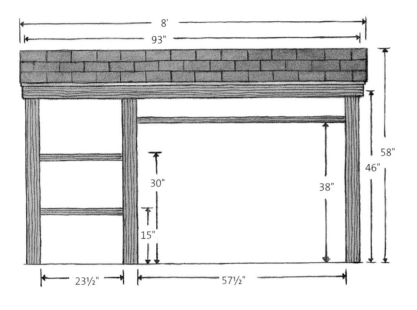

FINISHED SIZE 8 feet wide, 30 inches deep, 58 inches tall

Building a Recycle Center

1 To form a ledger board against the house, cut a 2 by 4 to measure 90 inches long. (Cut away sections of batten boards on the house wall, if necessary, to make space for the ledger.) To protect the house wall from moisture and termites, attach 6-inch-wide aluminum flashing where the ledger will be placed; use 1-inch roofing nails. With a helper, hold the ledger horizontally against the house wall so that its top is 58 inches above ground; check that the board is level. Attach the ledger to the house with deck screws.

Cut three 48-inch-long 2 by 4s for vertical supports against the house

wall. Again, protect wall with flashing. Using deck screws, attach two of the vertical supports under either end of ledger, allowing 1½ inches to extend beyond the ledger at each end; these extensions will support the outer two rafters. Fasten third support to house wall 2 feet from the inside edge of board on the left.

Dig three 18-inch-deep post holes, in line with the vertical boards on the house wall and 22¼ inches in front of the boards. (In climates where the ground freezes, deeper holes and longer posts may be required; check with your local building department.) Hold the posts in place with temporary bracing; check that they are square and

plumb. Mix the concrete and fill the holes with it, checking again to be sure the posts are square and plumb. Let the concrete cure for about 24 hours. Cut off the top of the center post at 46 inches above ground level. Cut the tops off the other two posts so they are level with the center post.

To make a top plate, cut two 2 by 4s to 93 inches each. With 8-penny nails, fasten them together across the top of the posts to support the rafters. Cut rafters from 2 by 4s. Make the two end rafters 30 inches long and the two middle ones 28½ inches long; rafters will overhang the top plate by 2 inches. (You may want to cut one 2 by 4 as a pattern for the rafters before cutting the others.) To make the rafter notches (also called bird's-mouths), either estimate the angles or use a framing square, following its tables and instructions. (You can also use rafter hangers instead of cutting notches to fit over the top plate.) Place the two end rafters on the vertical supports and nail them to the ledger board. Place one of the middle rafters over the top plate above the center post; set the other middle rafter 29 inches to the right of the first middle rafter. Toenail both to the ledger board and toenail all rafters to the top plate.

Cut seven pieces of 2 by 4 lumber, each 22¼ inches long, to make supports for the shelves. (Be sure all supports are level before nailing.)

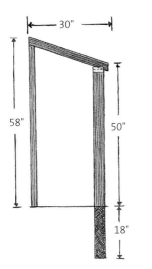

For the two shelves on the left side, toenail supports 15 inches and 30 inches above the ground between the inner edges of the posts and the vertical 2 by 4 supports on the house walls. For the shelf on the right side, attach supports 38 inches above ground. Nail the final 2 by 4 (used to strengthen the right side of the structure and to provide a surface on which to nail siding) 15 inches above ground.

2 Cut shelves from one 4- by 8-foot sheet of ½-inch plywood. Cut two shelves, each 31 inches wide and 22 inches deep; nail them to the supports. For the optional third shelf, cut a piece of plywood 65 inches wide and 18 inches deep; nail it to the supports.

For the roof, cut remaining 4- by 8-foot sheet of ½-inch plywood to measure 30 inches wide. Center it over the rafters and attach it in place with nails.

3 Attach roof flashing to the outer three edges of the plywood with 1-inch roofing nails. Staple roofing paper to the plywood and finish the roof with shingles or other roofing to match the house roof. Also finish both ends (here, ⅜-inch redwood siding and 2½-inch battens were used) and paint them. To conceal the rafters and to trim the top and bottom edges on each end, 3¼- by ⅝-inch redwood trim was used. To finish the front edge of each shelf, use 1¼-inch-wide, ¼-inch-thick strips of wood, cut to length; first glue them on, then nail them.

Add floor, if desired. Here, the owner continued an existing brick path, filling the joints between the bricks with fine sand.

MATERIALS & TOOLS 10 pressure-treated 2 by 4s, 8 feet long • 3 pressure-treated 4 by 4 posts, 8 feet long • 2 sheets ½-inch exterior plywood, 4 by 8 feet • 3 bags (50 pounds each) fast-setting concrete mix (post hole mix) • 20 feet aluminum flashing, 6 inches wide • 3½-inch deck screws • 1-inch roofing nails • 8-penny galvanized common nails • Rafter hangers (optional) • Post hole digger • Portable circular saw • Hand saw • Carpenter's level • Framing square (optional) • **Finishing materials:** 1¼- by ¼-inch strips of wood to edge shelves; glue; roofing (such as shingles); 30-pound roofing paper; staple gun; roof flashing; ⅜-inch-thick resawn redwood plywood siding; battens; 3¼- by ⅝-inch redwood trim; paint; bricks and fine sand for floor

Southern Exposure

A FEW TOUCHES of color and Southern comfort were all it took to transform a rather utilitarian entrance into a cheerful outdoor room for relaxing and entertaining. The change was mainly accomplished with hanging baskets of old-fashioned annual flowers and potted plants, and a fresh coat of sage-colored paint for the porch.

BEFORE

A Southern magnolia tucked in the corner in front of the porch had outgrown its tub, so it was planted out in the garden, making room for a bistro table and chairs. A pair of Victorian-style wire baskets on the porch rails and a hanging basket just under the eaves capture the sun without compromising the narrow space. Pots of flowers extend the garden onto the brick patio.

Antique baker's racks on the porch hold a collection of vintage garden ornaments and potted plants. The foliage of a fancy trumpet vine drapes over the windows like a living swag, creating a leafy green frame for the view of patio and porch from indoors.

CHALLENGE

The exposure was perfect for plantings, but the narrow porch and tiny patio had no room for a garden.

A heavy redwood box planted with a magnolia tree filled the only space available for a sitting area.

SOLUTION

Plants in pots and Victorian baskets decorate the entrance with bright flowers and trailing foliage.

An antique rocker on the porch and a table for two offer comfy places to sit a spell.

PLANT HIGHLIGHTS

Blue star creeper
Pratia pedunculata

Ivy
Hedera helix

Ivy geranium
Pelargonium peltatum

Lobelia

Million bells
Calibrachoa

Baby-faced Basket

A HANGING BASKET of shade-tolerant plants strikes just the right cheerful note on the side porch, making nice use of the narrow space between the door and the window.

Baby's tears serves as the basket's living liner, creating a green pocket for pastel fuchsia and campanula blooms, the ruffled fronds of a bird's nest fern, and the colorful variegated foliage of a fancy rex begonia.

To water the basket, the gardener takes it down, props it against the porch steps, and drenches it with water. She allows it to drain thoroughly before hanging it back up.

FOR THE LINER, PURCHASE PLANTS IN A MUDFLAT, WHICH IS A PLASTIC NURSERY FLAT WITHOUT DIVIDERS. IF YOUR NURSERY DOES NOT STOCK MUDFLATS, THE STAFF CAN ORDER THEM FOR YOU.

Lining a Wire Basket with Ground Cover

1 Cut a piece of coco-fiber liner or cardboard to fit inside the flat back of the half-basket (the part that will be against the wall). Set the back of the basket diagonally on the mudflat, with its lower corner near a corner of the mudflat. With a knife, trim away the top corner of the ground cover flush with the top of the basket.

2 Remove the larger portion of the ground cover from flat (save the top corner for another use). Set it inside basket with the leafy side against front of basket, facing out. The top edge of the ground cover should be flush with the top of the basket; the bottom corner should fit into the bottom. Press the ground cover against the front of basket.

3 Pour potting mix into a bucket and moisten it; mix in fertilizer in the amount directed on the package. Fill the basket three-fourths full with the potting mix. Set the fern in the center of the basket; place the other plants around it. Firm the potting mix around the root balls and water thoroughly. Hang the basket in partial shade. Keep soil moist.

MATERIALS & TOOLS 16-inch wire half-basket • Piece of coco-fiber liner or cardboard • 1 cubic foot potting mix • Controlled-release fertilizer • One 16-inch-square mudflat baby's tears or other ground cover, such as blue star creeper, chamomile, creeping thyme, or Irish moss • One 6-inch pot bird's nest fern • One 4-inch pot rex begonia with deep-colored foliage • One 4- or 6-inch pot pink fuchsia • One 4-inch pot other flowering plant suited to hanging baskets (shown here is hybrid campanula 'Wonder Bells Blue') • Knife • Bucket

Tropical Twist

A NEGLECTED SIDE YARD took a turn for the tropical when the owners decided to rescue the narrow (just 18- by 70-foot) space and put it to good use. Working with a landscape designer, they discovered there was plenty of room to lay down a generous stone patio

BEFORE

and, at the top of a short flight of stairs, a small terrace outside new living room doors. The flagstone paving ties the two areas together visually. A splashing fountain on the upper terrace mutes the traffic noise from outside the garden.

To make the space seem larger, the dining patio just outside the kitchen was set at a 45-degree angle to the house and the new garden walls. The angular flower beds in the garden are at most about 3 feet wide, but they are packed with tropical plants bearing bright flowers and dramatic foliage that invite close inspection.

PLANT HIGHLIGHTS

Angel's trumpet
Brugmansia versicolor
'Charles Grimaldi'

Begonia (tuberous)

Black elder
Sambucus nigra 'Madonna'

Canna hybrids

Honey bush
Melianthus major

Princess flower
Tibouchina urvilleana

Owners needed an area for outdoor entertaining.

Available space in the side yard was limited to a narrow strip.

SOLUTION

A new stone patio provides the perfect space for dining and entertaining.

Setting the patio at an angle to the house and using colorful, bold-foliaged plants makes the small side yard seem much larger.

71

Gaining
Ground

Lithe and Lush

LEFT: The curly straw-colored leaves of sedge look like party streamers among the blooms in a cheerful flower pot on a front porch. Long-lasting strawflowers and tall zinnias act as supports for the sedge; petunias and geraniums whirl around the rim of the pot.

Silvery Simplicity

ABOVE: Red geraniums and silvery licorice plant decorate the wrought-iron railings around a balcony, putting on a sophisticated show for passersby. The plants don't mind the close quarters of a window box, and they flourish with little attention.

Light and Lacy

BELOW: Compact white zinnias, silvery artemisia, and wispy bronze-leafed sedge make an elegant little garden in a 14-inch pot. Artemisia and sedge are perennials; after a season, transplant them to a permanent place in a garden bed.

Double Decker

ABOVE: A large flower pot is nested into another to make a split-level container in this kitchen garden. Lemon grass sprays up from the center of the top pot; ornamental sweet potato vine trails around the edges of the bottom one.

Lunch is served in a secluded corner of a leafy patio. An attractive retaining wall was built into a hillside to create this comfortable outdoor room; recycled timbers were used in the trellis overhead. A wall fountain and antique corbels add touches of romance and old-world charm.

Light Fantastic

RIGHT: A trellis covered with vines shades this patio by day. In the evening, rows of tiny lights on the trellis add subtle spatial definition and a bit of sparkle to the cozy space. The border between indoors and out is nearly invisible.

In the Pink

BELOW: Matching green rockers provide a welcome rest stop in this narrow patio. By keeping the plant palette simple and balancing the arrangement carefully, this gardener managed to display a dozen different pots around the table. Two cape mallow plants bloom almost at eye level behind the chairs.

Personal Paradise

ANYTHING GOES IN THE BACKYARD. This is the gardener's private domain, where the only rule is: please yourself.

All the parts of this small backyard were well defined, but the lawn isolated them from each other; there was no flow from the back door to the flower beds or the patio. Working with a landscape designer, the owners reorganized the space, making the lawn smaller to allow room for a wide gravel path that wraps around the garden. Lanky rose bushes and an overgrown camellia were taken out and replaced with a lively mix of low-maintenance perennials. Now flowers and foliage spill softly over the edges of the planting beds.

Decorative antique trellises were installed against the wall of the house and the neighbors' garage, helping to break up the stark expanse—and giving the garden the feel of a tranquil old-world courtyard.

BEFORE

What is paradise? But a garden, an orchard of trees, and herbs full of pleasure and nothing there but delights.

—WILLIAM LAWSON

CHALLENGE

The short walk off the back porch led right into a wall, and there was no defined access to planting beds.

A big camellia blocked the view; scraggly plants didn't suit their locations.

SOLUTION

A flowing path surrounds the garden, smoothly linking all the parts.

Billowy, lower-growing plants soften the back entry and open up the view.

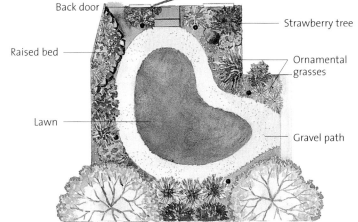

Back door

Strawberry tree

Raised bed

Ornamental grasses

Lawn

Gravel path

A Streaming Gravel Path

A STRONG DESIGN is the foundation of every beautiful garden, and convenient and graceful paths are crucial elements of that design. At this home, the owners walked out their back door onto a brick landing and then felt stranded: there was no walkway to lead them from the paved area to the flower beds or the patio.

To solve the problem, they removed the bricks and designed a new gravel path that curves around the garden, allowing a close approach to every bed. A paisley-shaped sweep of lawn in the center looks all the greener and gives the small area a feeling of spaciousness.

TIP

IN BOTH MATERIALS AND

DESIGN, PATHS SHOULD

REFLECT THE GARDEN'S STYLE

AND YOUR NEEDS. A CURVING

GRAVEL PATH LOOKS RELAXED;

A STRAIGHT BRICK WALK IS

MORE FORMAL.

1

2

3

Installing a Gravel Path

1 Mark the outline of the path with powdered limestone or gypsum. Remove sod and excavate soil to a depth of 4 inches. (If desired, reserve some of the soil to fill the raised bed described on page 80.)

Flexible and long lasting, benderboard is ideal for edging paths with gentle curves; for strength, use layers of two or three boards. This path's border is made with 8-foot lengths of benderboard. Wet the benderboard to make it more supple. Then lay out two pieces end to end on a flat surface. Center a third piece over the junction of the first two and attach it in several places with small wood

screws. To complete one end of the edging, cut a 4-foot length of benderboard and attach it on one side of the centered piece.

Drive stakes along the outside edge of the path, spacing them 2 to 4 feet apart; use the closer spacing on curves. The top of each stake should be the same height above ground as the top edge of the benderboard. With a helper, lay the section of benderboard edging in place and attach it to the stakes with screws. Continue to add layered sections of benderboard until you reach the end of the path. For extra support, drive more stakes (2 to 4 feet apart) along the inside of the benderboard edging; the tops of

these stakes should be an inch below the top edge of the benderboard, so that they'll be covered by the gravel topcoat. Screw the stakes to the benderboard.

Repeat to edge the other side of the path with benderboard.

2 Place landscape fabric over the path to help prevent the growth of weeds, tucking it firmly under the edges of the benderboard. Spread 2 inches of base rock or crushed gravel over the fabric. Sprinkle rock lightly with water to dampen it; then tamp it in place to make a level, firm foundation.

3 Add a 2-inch-deep gravel topcoat and rake to make it smooth and level. To keep the gravel looking tidy, rake it periodically.

MATERIALS & TOOLS Powdered limestone or gypsum • Lengths of benderboard, 8 feet long by 4 inches wide • 1 by 2 stakes, 1 foot long • Wood screws • Landscape fabric • Base rock or crushed gravel • Gravel for topcoat, such as pea gravel • Tamper

TIP

AS YOU BUILD THE RAISED BED, KEEP A PILE OF SMALL STONES NEARBY; WEDGE THEM BETWEEN ANY UNSTABLE STONES TO PREVENT WOBBLING AND MAKE THE BED'S WALL STRONGER. THEY ARE ALSO USEFUL FOR FILLING LARGER CRACKS BETWEEN STONES. SEE PAGE 143 FOR INFORMA-TION ON BUILDING A DRY-STACKED STONE WALL ALONG A GENTLE SLOPE.

Building a Dry-stacked Stone Wall

1 Dig a trench 4 to 6 inches deep to help hold the first layer of stones in place. Pile the soil nearby.

2 Place stones in the trench, selecting the larger stones for the first layer. Place more stones on top of and between them to make a wall about a foot high. Set in stones as securely as possible, trying to fit them together snugly.

Mix compost with the reserved soil from the trench. (If you have constructed the gravel path on page 79 and have extra soil from this, add some of it as well.) Use this amended soil to fill the raised bed; pack some soil between stones for additional planting pockets.

Set taller-growing plants at the back of the bed (or at its center, if you have built a free-standing bed). Plant lower growers to spill over the edges and fill in among the stones.

MATERIALS & TOOLS Stones • Compost (bagged or homemade)

Details Make a Difference

WELL-PLACED ORNAMENTS of all kinds add the finishing touches that give a garden its personality and charm. Natural decorations, such as large stones or interestingly shaped pieces of driftwood, introduce dramatic contrasts in flower beds. Antique garden ornaments lend a sense of history—even if you use them for a different purpose than was originally intended.

ABOVE: **The antique trellises in the garden may once have served as sections of a fence.**

RIGHT: **A large rock in a flower bed contrasts dramatically with the blooms around it and with the delicate ironwork of a trellis on the wall behind it.**

BELOW: **Terra-cotta sconces mounted on the fence and planted with purple-leafed basil and other herbs bring the garden up to eye level.**

Rounding off the Edges

RETIREMENT CHANGED this owner's feelings about her backyard. Suddenly, now that she had time to appreciate it, the space wasn't good enough: it lacked charm, the angles were too sharp, and the plants all seemed dull. With the help of a landscape designer, she redefined the area, replacing

BEFORE

rigid straight lines with gentle curves, and added ample plantings of flowers.

The new garden revolves around an oval lawn outlined neatly with bricks. A graceful gravel path sweeps between the lawn and a densely planted mixed border. A line of rocks along the edge of the gravel is reminiscent of a stream bank, giving the path the illusion of movement.

Tall trees shelter the space, but as the sun moves over the leafy canopy, it throws sparkling, shifting spotlights on the flowers in the garden below.

PLANT HIGHLIGHTS

Blueberry

Delphinium

Flowering currant
Ribes sanguineum

Rhododendron

Rose

Vine maple
Acer circinatum

CHALLENGE

Large, rectangular lawn marginalized garden area and plantings.

Unplanned, sparsely planted garden lacked personality and charm.

SOLUTION

A smaller, gently curving lawn and generous gravel path create an easy, comfortable flow through the garden.

Plantings with graceful foliage and bright flowers create an enchanting woodland feel; the densely planted borders add rich texture.

The Plot Thickens

A SUNNY PATCH OF GROUND used as a makeshift vegetable plot was transformed into a colorful cutting garden in this backyard. The space was too small to produce a satisfying crop of vegetables, but now that it's devoted exclusively to annual and perennial flowers, it provides blooms for bouquets all summer long.

BEFORE

The new garden seems much larger than the old one. A flagstone path that came to a dead end behind the original plot was extended around the garden and now leads to a shady seating area; a shorter path divides the planting into two sections. The walkways make it easier to reach the flowers for tending and gathering—and just admiring close up.

The exuberant garden is edged with willow whips, woven together into a low, neat border that makes a pretty frame for the flowers and holds up tall stems around the perimeter of the plot. If you can't find flexible willow branches, any low, natural-looking boundary will work just as well.

PLANT HIGHLIGHTS

Baby's breath
Gypsophila paniculata

Black-eyed Susan
Rudbeckia fulgida sullivantii
'Goldsturm'

Cosmos

Floss flower
Ageratum houstonianum

Lisianthus
Eustoma grandiflorum

Purple coneflower
Echinacea purpurea 'Magnus'

CHALLENGE

A tired vegetable garden offered only a limited harvest, and the plot was an eyesore for much of the year.

Dead-end path didn't extend into the garden for caretaking.

SOLUTION

A striking cutting garden offers a generous harvest of fresh cut flowers throughout the summer.

Extended path goes through and around the garden and even leads to a shady rest area.

Sitting area

Lavender

Purple coneflower

Flagstone path

Cosmos

Twig trellis

Twig edging

Floss flower

Roses

A Shady Corner

MOST FLOWERS PREFER a place in the sun, but many gardeners would rather enjoy the bright colors from a shady and comfortable spot. All that's needed is an overhanging, leafy limb and a space large enough for a table and a chair.

This elegant fan-back wicker chair and matching table fit neatly into a corner just off a flagstone path. A white-glazed water pitcher is stuffed full of the garden's own flowers, so the gardener can appreciate them up close. The big chair isn't heavy: it can come inside or move outdoors, depending on the weather.

TIP

INDOOR FURNITURE LOOKS

BOLD AND NEW IN THE GARDEN.

TAKE AN ANTIQUE ROCKER

OUTSIDE FOR THE AFTERNOON,

OR MOVE A MODERN SETTEE

TO THE PATIO FOR A PARTY.

OPPOSITE: **Take as much as you want: ready-to-cut bouquets are the benefit of a cutting garden.**

RIGHT: **The gardener made a tidy edging by cutting willow wands into uniform lengths and weaving them together all the way around the garden. Zinnias and salvia grow through the little fence, blurring the boundaries.**

BELOW RIGHT: **Longer willow sticks were used to make a 4-foot tepee for bright pink morning glories. The tension of the bent twigs is all that's needed to hold the structure together.**

BELOW: **A pair of little wren houses are used as decorative finials at the tops of 4 by 4 posts. The posts serve as sturdy hose guards at the corners of planting beds.**

Kitchen Herb Garden

HERB GARDENS have to be close to the kitchen door, but when the door opens onto the back stairs, there's no place to plant. This gardener solved the problem by planting everything in containers. It's hard to grow herbs closer to the soup pot than this.

A collection of old sap buckets and other containers made from salvaged materials gives the

BEFORE

setting the charm of a country garden. Biscuit tins, old teakettles, and other antique finds are all fine containers, as long as you make drainage holes in them before planting. Thyme, oregano, sage, parsley, mint, and basil don't mind being crowded in their pots, and they thrive in the sunny spot. It's easy to remember to care for them as you come and go. The most essential herbs grow in a pot on a weathered bench at one side of the door, which is decorated with a wreath of bay leaves. A columnar apple tree stands sentry on the other side.

CHALLENGE

The owners wanted an herb garden near the kitchen door, but no ground was available for planting.

Porch decking was unfinished and humdrum.

SOLUTION

Containers overflowing with edible plants and fruit now fill the bill for the kitchen garden.

The porch was painted a soft bluish gray to complement the house colors and the new herb garden.

PLANT HIGHLIGHTS

Columnar apple

Garden sage
Salvia officinalis 'Icterina'

Oregano
Origanum vulgare

Rosemary
Rosmarinus officinalis

Silver thyme
Thymus vulgaris 'Argenteus'

Viola

88

A New View

THIS PATHWAY didn't flow: the concrete walk cut off abruptly, and the straggling line of concrete pavers tacked on beyond it looked like an afterthought. To bring the setting into focus, the owners laid a brick path and put a gate that's purely for show at the far property line.

The new path emphasizes the balance and symmetry in the garden. Although the red gate, with its blue-gray posts, is just for looks, it's a natural focal point that enhances the view and plantings around it.

90

BEFORE

TIP BEFORE BUILDING THIS PATH'S BORDER, LAY OUT A SAMPLE SECTION OF THE BRICK PATTERN. THAT WAY, YOU CAN CHOOSE A PATH WIDTH THAT WILL SAVE YOU FROM HAVING TO CUT TOO MANY BRICKS TO SIZE. DIRECTIONS FOR CONSTRUCTING A MORTARED BRICK BORDER ARE GIVEN ON PAGES 13–14.

Laying Brick in Sand

1 Excavate the path area (plus 6 inches on either side) to a depth of 4 inches and make the mortared brick border. Then spread 2 inches of base rock or crushed gravel over path. Tamp to make a level, firm base. Lay landscape fabric over the gravel to prevent weed growth. Top with a 2-inch layer of dampened sand. To level the sand and make a smooth surface for the bricks, pull a strike board between the borders.

2 Set a piece of plywood on the path; kneel on this as you work to minimize disturbance to the sand base. Starting from one corner, set the bricks in position, making sure they fit as planned. Lightly tap each brick into place with a rubber mallet or the end of a hammer handle. Check level as you work; if a brick is too low, pry it out and add more sand. Wear eye protection.

3 Sweep fine sand into the joints between bricks. (The coarse sand used as a base will not fit as smoothly between bricks.) Wet the area with a light spray to settle the sand completely. If necessary, sweep in more sand and dampen again.

MATERIALS & TOOLS You will need the materials listed on page 13 (not including flagstones) plus the following: 1 by 4 lumber • Piece of plywood • Base rock or crushed gravel • Fine sand • Rubber mallet

Making a Screed Board

Also called a strike board, a screed board is used to level sand between edgings. Cut a 1 by 4 piece of lumber several inches longer than the total width of the path. Nail on another 1 by 4 board, cut to fit between the inside edges of the mortared brick border; it should extend below the first board by slightly less than the thickness of one brick (typically $2^3/8$ inches).

Upscale Garden

IT TOOK THE OWNERS of this garden two years to complete the job of taking out a lap pool they did not want and creating a new stone terrace where the pool had been. A landscape architect helped them develop the plans, but they did all the work themselves.

BEFORE

Once the difficult, backbreaking task of removing the pool was done, they built a patio with weathered stones from a salvage yard, leaving enough space against the fence enclosing the sunny terrace for a vegetable garden in a large raised bed. They edged the bed with broken concrete and installed trellises for peas at the back. Tulips bloom in the new bed in spring; as soon as the weather warms up, the flowers are replaced with tomatoes and other vegetables.

Chamomile and thyme bloom between the stones of the terrace; unthirsty, shade-loving plants happily hug the hillside. A cozy seating area offers a pretty upslope view.

PLANT HIGHLIGHTS

Common calla
Zantedeschia aethiopica

Daffodil
Narcissus

Hosta

Magnolia

Tulip
Tulipa

Woolly thyme
Thymus pseudolanuginosus

CHALLENGE

A large lap pool occupied the only sunny, level space in the backyard.

Overgrown trees and shrubs didn't suit the space and slope conditions.

SOLUTION

A stone terrace bordered with mixed perennials and small trees and shrubs replaces the pool.

The hillside plantings thrive in the dry shade and help prevent soil erosion.

Meadow Magic

MAINTAINING A TRADITIONAL lawn in this small backyard was a struggle, so the owner decided to replace it with a low-maintenance meadow of fragrant chamomile, low-growing sedges, and fine-textured fescues. The ragged little yard has now become an inviting refuge. The grasses need occasional shearing, but their colors and textures blend

BEFORE

to create a naturally shaggy ground cover that appears to be the work of nature.

Daylilies pop up like wayside wild-flowers through the grasses at the front of the meadow. Self-sufficient perennials, as informal as the grasses, are planted here and there around the edges of the garden.

A small pond, neglected in a shady corner of the garden, was a nuisance—attractive to bugs and popular with raccoons, who came there at night to forage and stayed to dig up chunks of turf from the lawn. The owner replaced it with a quietly bubbling fountain, as subtle as the setting.

PLANT HIGHLIGHTS

Chamomile
Chamaemelum nobile

Daylily
Hemerocallis hybrids

Fescues, blue and red
Festuca glauca and *F. rubra*

Rudbeckia
Rudbeckia fulgida sullivantii
'Goldsturm'

Sedge (variegated)
Carex albula 'Frosty Curls'

CHALLENGE

The lawn was patchy and difficult to maintain; the backyard was soggy on one side, dry on the other.

Standing water in the pond lured mosquitoes and other pests to the garden.

SOLUTION

The former lawn is now a lush meadow of grasses and wildflowers.

New seating and the sound of trickling water from the fountain create a peaceful place for quiet reflection.

Stone fountain   Bench   Bamboo screen

Feather reed grass

Black-eyed Susan

Sedge

Daylily   Chamomile

DO IT TODAY

A Refreshing Retreat

STEAL AWAY to a park bench in your own backyard, and the noise and hubbub of the world seem to disappear.

A gently curving line of slate stepping-stones defines an informal patio in the midst of the cool meadow grasses in this little yard. An antique bench with a new folding table painted to match offers the perfect place to enjoy a cup of coffee and read the morning paper.

In one quiet corner of the yard, a trickling fountain is surrounded by perennials with ferny and grassy foliage. A painted ceramic statue stands amid the bamboo, keeping a friendly eye on the scene.

TIP

SELECT STONES WITH ONE FLAT SIDE. LARGER STONES (A FOOT OR MORE ACROSS) ARE EASIER TO LEVEL AND LESS LIKELY TO WOBBLE. USE THE SOD YOU REMOVE TO PATCH BARE SPOTS IN THE LAWN.

96

1

2

Setting Stones in Sod

1 Place the stones on the lawn, moving them as needed to create a pleasing arrangement and spacing them closely enough to make a path that's easy to walk on. With a sharp spade, cut the outline of each stone in the sod. Remove each stone and dig out the sod, making a hole that conforms as closely as possible to the bottom of the stone.

2 Place about half a shovelful of sand in each hole to help level and settle the stones. Replace the stones, setting them firmly into the sand. The top of each stone should be level with the surrounding lawn, allowing a lawn mower to travel over the stone. If necessary, add or remove sand to help level the stones.

MATERIALS & TOOLS Stones • Coarse or builder's sand • Sharp spade

BEFORE

ABOVE: **Before, the still water of a pond attracted mosquitoes and other pests to the garden.**
RIGHT: **Recirculating water spills gently from the new fountain.**

Cool Country Charm

WHEN THIS GARDENER'S CHILDREN grew up and left home, she decided to claim their old badminton court—the backyard—for herself. A lawn wouldn't be necessary, she decided; the new garden just needed paths to draw the eye into the space, and an attractive flight of steps leading to the upper terrace. A boggy spot also needed some attention.

BEFORE

A wide gravel terrace took the place of the back lawn, and flowering perennials of all kinds were planted in front of the low wall and in the colorful new garden at the top of the stairs. Stepping-stones on the terrace lead to a bench tucked under an old apple tree. Moisture-loving Japanese irises now thrive in the wet spot.

Although the bench beckons, the bright blue stairs have become the owner's favorite place to sit in her new garden.

PLANT HIGHLIGHTS

Chrysanthemum

Columbine
Aquilegia

Japanese iris
Iris ensata hybrid

Phlox

Pussy willow (weeping)
Salix caprea

High-maintenance lawn was no longer appealing.

The garden needed a path and focal point to tie areas together.

A handsome gravel terrace replaces the lawn.

Attractive blue bench and matching blue steps draw the eye into the new perennial garden.

Magic &
Special
Effects

Picture
Perfect

The best gardens combine art
and nature into a beautiful,
seamless whole. In this garden,
jagged rocks, carefully raked
gravel, and a dogwood tree at
the height of bloom eloquently
express the transience and
drama of the season.

Elegant
Simplicity

RIGHT: **This garden puts simple principles to work: it relies on an intense play of textures to create excitement and interest, without a single touch of flower color. Swirling patterns on the rocks suggest the flow of water.**

Sitting
Pretty

BELOW: **Thyme, oregano, rosemary, and parsley sit comfortably in an old chair fitted with a hanging basket. The weathered chair appears to have a long new life ahead of it in the garden.**

Silly Safari

BELOW: **Deep in the greenery, a fanciful red giraffe seems to munch contentedly on the leaves of a birch tree. In the winter, after the hostas die back and the birch leaves fall, the shiny red creature stands out even more brightly.**

New Attitude

ABOVE: The owners of this garden replaced their thirsty lawn with a sophisticated combination of drought-tolerant perennials. Now a gravel path winds artfully through an exuberant mix of Japanese silver grass, Japanese blood grass, lavender blue spiraea, silvery lamb's ears, and artemisia. The narrowing path makes the garden seem much larger than it is.

Crazy Feet

RIGHT: Old running shoes get a new life as stepping-stones on a garden path that disappears around a large butterfly bush. There is at least one season of life left in these durable old soles.

Grand Finale

RIGHT: **A charming late-season combination of soft apricot roses, porcelain berry vine, and goldenrod surrounds this painted fence post. This may be an unplanned autumn bouquet, but it's perfectly all right to give yourself the credit for it.**

Branching Out

BELOW: **Gnarled, nubby branches are the essence of rustic furniture, which became popular in the early 19th century. In this modern garden, a pair of magnificent driftwood chairs carries on the romantic rustic tradition.**

Secret Garden

ABOVE: **Unpainted Dutch doors in an adobe wall open to an inviting patio. The owners haven't shied away from color: the doors are painted bright blue on the inside, and pink, orange, and red flowers spill from terra-cotta pots.**

Still Life

ABOVE: A paintbrush and a lot of imagination transformed a tall, blank wall into a tropical forest giant sheltering parrots, a monkey, and a bright, bejeweled red gecko. Ice plants drape down from pots at the top of the wall, bringing the tree to life. LEFT: A treasured piece of sculpture deserves special treatment: this Indonesian bust is displayed on a beautifully hewn stone pillar. Behind it, an exuberant perennial garden is in full summer flower. There's a delicate tension between the excitement of the ephemeral flowers and the ageless countenance lost in thought.

What Mirror Where?

RIGHT: Mirrors—like water—reflect light around the garden and add a bit of mystery to the setting. Here, an oval mirror draws a quiet gleam into a dark corner and seems to extend the garden well beyond the shadows.

A Blue Mood

BELOW RIGHT: Luminous blue globes of all sizes and shapes dominate this decorating scheme. The spheres are everywhere: arranged on the ground like a cluster of mushrooms, suspended on poles, hanging from the trees. A gigantic blue dragonfly flits among them.

Tooleries

BELOW: Even when these rakes began losing their teeth, the gardener still loved them. She assembled a huge bouquet of them beside a potting shed, right behind a clump of bronze-foliaged cannas. An ancient shovel juts from one side of the arrangement.

Urban Retreats

USUALLY SMALL SPACES, PATIOS AND BALCONIES challenge a gardener's resourcefulness. To make the most of them, you have to be creative: a limited space naturally narrows the landscaping possibilities and the number of guests who can comfortably enjoy the area.

This tiny patio—only about 4 feet wide and 15 feet long—is surrounded on three sides by the tall, irregular staves of a fence made from old grape trellises, which provides an interesting backdrop and allows some light to come through. The gardener took advantage of all the available space by using containers, hanging baskets, a trellis, and shelving for plantings. The bright blooms of a flowering maple against the fence attract hummingbirds to this urban haven. A backlit forest of bonsai trees, in perfect scale with the diminutive space, is arranged on a handsome slatted shelf that runs along the fence.

Not wholly in the busy world, not quite beyond it, blooms the garden that I love.

—TENNYSON

BEFORE

CHALLENGE

Exposed aggregate floor, bare wooden fencing, and a shady exposure added up to a dull, dark space.

Only a ribbon of soil was available for in-ground planting.

SOLUTION

Shade-loving plants with variegated foliage and light-colored blooms brighten the patio.

Containers filled with lush plantings extend garden space and improve the look of patio floor and fence.

ABOVE: **A stand of bonsai trees on a shelf adds a new dimension to the garden.**

A Bonsai Retreat

A BRIGHT BLUE CHAIR invites the gardener to escape for a few moments from the busy world outside, but there's competition for such a cozy spot: when the owner isn't looking, his cat loves to curl up on the comfortable cushion.

A multilevel garden of choice plants in pots and hanging baskets envelops the quiet corner. The chair was a garage-sale find, revived with a coat of enamel. The metal box beside it contains potting soil but also serves as a side table. On the tabletop is a Kurume azalea bonsai in bloom, a striking miniature specimen.

TIP

TO CREATE A MOSSY CARPET UNDER BONSAI, SPRINKLE DRIED, POWDERED MOSS (FROM A NURSERY) OVER THE MOIST SOIL, TAMP IN PLACE, AND WATER FREQUENTLY WITH A FINE MIST.

Creating a Bonsai

1 To prevent soil from washing out of the bonsai dish, cut two 2-inch-square pieces of plastic mesh and lay one over each drainage hole on the inside of the dish. To fasten each piece of mesh in place, make two loops in a 4-inch-long piece of wire and slip ends through the mesh and drainage hole. Turn the dish over and bend the wire outward.

2 To make anchors to hold the plant's root ball in place, begin by cutting the heads off the matchsticks. Set two of them aside. Then cut two 20-inch lengths of wire. Center one of the remaining matchsticks on each length of wire; wind wire six times around matchstick.

Cut two 3-inch-long pieces of wire and bend each in half. Attach a wired matchstick to the inside of each drainage hole by placing another (non-wired) matchstick on the outside of the drainage hole and slipping the ends of the short wire over the wired matchstick, through the mesh and the hole, and around the outer matchstick; twist the ends tightly (photo 2a). Anchor-wires extend upward from the inside of the dish (photo 2b).

3 Half-fill the dish with potting mix, leaving the anchor-wires exposed. Remove the azalea from its pot. Prune away a few of the branches to thin out the top growth, making the plant's structure more open and treelike.

Carefully ease the soil away from the roots and gently untangle them; mist the roots frequently with water while you work. Cut off two-thirds of the roots, flattening the bottom of the root ball and rounding the sides. The pruned and flattened root ball should cover about two-thirds of the surface area of the bonsai dish; the depth of the root mass should be one-third to one-half the depth of the dish.

Position the base of the plant in the dish just off center. Add potting mix to hold the root ball in place, working it in and around the plant's roots with a chopstick.

4 To anchor the root ball firmly, cut two 3/4- by 4-inch-long strips from the remaining plastic mesh. Lay a strip across each side of the root ball. Pull an anchor-wire through narrow ends of each piece of mesh, then twist ends of wire together across the mesh. Clip off excess wire. Finish filling the pot with potting mix. Water well.

MATERIALS & TOOLS 6-inch-square piece of plastic mesh screen • Bonsai dish, approximately 11 inches long by 6½ inches wide • 24-gauge copper or aluminum wire • 4 sturdy wooden matchsticks or four 2-inch-long pieces of ⅛-inch-thick wood • Potting soil • Azalea in 1-gallon container • Wire cutters • Pruners • Spray bottle • Chopstick

Setting the Stage for Relaxation

A LITTLE WORK and a few deft decorating touches changed this plain slab patio into an exciting outdoor room. The bland garage wall wasn't very friendly; the Adirondack chairs and table were in good shape but didn't really suit the mood the owners had in mind. To create a fresh look, they painted the wall a rich butterscotch and replaced the furniture with a plantation teak rocker and chaise, plumped up with pillows and cushions.

BEFORE

A straw mat hides the concrete slab's flaws and defines the space just as an area rug does indoors. The inexpensive mat is comfortable underfoot and should last a year or more on the patio. A small striped throw rug under the table adds a warm indoor touch to the scene. Dramatic plants in glazed pots subtly enclose the seating area under a big blue market umbrella. Now the patio has the sunny charm of a Caribbean cabana.

CHALLENGE

The plain stucco wall and harsh gray concrete floor made the patio uninviting.

The unshaded space was glaring and uncomfortably hot; drab unfinished furniture lacked character and appeal.

SOLUTION

The lively golden wall, soft wheat-colored mat, and colorful accents and plants create an appealing outdoor room.

With its large sapphire umbrella and attractive, comfortable seating, the patio is now a favorite spot for reading and relaxing.

110

Coloring Outside the Lines

A BOXED-IN PATIO looked more like a parking spot than a relaxing refuge until great design ideas brought the space to life.

The squares of pavement were stained a sandy brown and edged in a darker brown to soften their harshness and complement the brick home. Ferns billowing from a pair of iron urns on either side of the French doors impart an old-fashioned,

BEFORE

urbane formality. In a corner, a still pool draws light down into the shady garden, and impatiens and other bright annuals make splashes of color. To add more greenery without giving up precious space, the gardener mounted a rustic trellis against the wall of the house and installed a wide, sturdy shelf around the top of the existing fence. White-leafed caladiums glow at eye level in planters on the shelf.

For step-by-step instructions on acid-staining concrete, see page 51.

Narrow strips of soil were the only planting areas available.

Glaring white concrete made the space look harsh and sterile.

SOLUTION

Containers, a trellis, and shelves on the fence add planting space.

Tinting mellows the concrete's glare, helping to blend the flooring with the house and garden.

PLANT HIGHLIGHTS

Cast-iron plant
Aspidistra elatior

Fancy-leafed caladium
Caladium bicolor

Holly fern
Cyrtomium falcatum

Impatiens
New Guinea hybrids

Japanese aucuba
Aucuba japonica

Applied Geometry

THIS URBAN BACKYARD didn't seem to offer the owners many possibilities until they shopped around for a house with something better. When they couldn't find what they wanted, they came home ready to give their property another chance. They have now created a woodsy, private garden with a patio and pond just outside the French doors

BEFORE

of their dining room.

One of the owners, a landscape designer, sketched an octagon in the lawn where the pond would be, and then repeated the form to define an outdoor dining area. The two octagons are also linked visually by a quiltlike pattern of fieldstones. A section of the pond extending back almost to the fence contains a bubbling fountain made from a birdbath. All around the margins of the garden, shade-loving perennials and shrubs thrive in a dense and subtle tapestry of green and golden foliage.

PLANT HIGHLIGHTS

Creeping Jenny
Lysimachia nummularia 'Aurea'

Epimedium

Fountain bamboo
Fargesia nitida

Fuchsia
Fuchsia triphylla 'Gartenmeister Bonstedt'

Mrs. Robb's bonnet
Euphorbia amygdaloides robbiae

Sedge
Carex elata 'Aurea'

CHALLENGE

The plain yard didn't have a comfortable outdoor living area.

Existing garden plantings offered no privacy from neighbors.

SOLUTION

A new patio extends living space to the outdoors. A deep border of shade-loving plants frames the fieldstone patio and pond and creates a view.

Garden "woods" now shield the new patio from the neighbors' view.

From Garage to Garden

THE OWNERS OF THIS PROPERTY borrowed space from their garage to make a welcoming patio garden right outside the kitchen door. They turned the front of the garage into a narrow sun porch with French doors, added a pergola over a stone terrace, and moved the driveway and garage door to the back.

BEFORE

Guests now park in a new space in front of the house and are welcomed in through the garden gate.

Sunny flower beds on both sides of the picket fence around the terrace soon became the owners' favorite place to plant. When the weather is pleasant, the family has breakfast, lunch, and dinner outdoors.

A silver lace vine quickly covered the pergola with a cloak of glossy leaves and frothy cream-white blooms, filtering the light that shines into the sun room. A swing on the eaves under the pergola isn't just for looks. The family has a rule: whoever comes home first gets the swing.

PLANT HIGHLIGHTS

Fancy-leafed caladium
Caladium bicolor

Hinoki false cypress
Chamaecyparis obtusa

Sage
Salvia nemorosa

Silver lace vine
Fallopia baldschuanica

Sunflower
Helianthus

Verbena hybrids

116

CHALLENGE

The entry wasn't welcoming; guests had to walk up the driveway and enter through the kitchen.

Old foundation plants were handsome, but left little room for new plantings.

SOLUTION

Garden gates invite visitors onto a flowery terrace; a sun porch outside the kitchen adds living space.

The new terrace offers ample room for plants in a variety of textures and colors.

A Seacoast Terrace in the Treetops

A DRAMATIC VIEW calls for plants with some stage presence. This balcony garden looked like an afterthought until the gardener decided to expand and improve the plant selection and create a fresh-air living space. The result doesn't interfere with the view, but transforms a rather stark balcony into a comfortable and inviting aerie.

BEFORE

A bistro table and chairs nestled among the plants give this narrow balcony the illusion of depth. Succulents, fan palms, and coast rosemary were chosen for year-round interest and for their adaptability to containers and to the seaside conditions. The glazed and unglazed terracotta pots are informally arranged, inviting the gardener to reposition the containers and plants through the seasons. Indoors, a collection of houseplants arranged in front of the large windows creates an effortless visual transition to the balcony.

PLANT HIGHLIGHTS

Coast rosemary
Westringia fruticosa

Crassula falcata

Haworthia attenuata

Hen and chicks
Echeveria elegans

Mediterranean fan palm
Chamaerops humilis

New Zealand flax
Phormium tenax

Stark, narrow balcony detracted from the seacoast view.

Few plants survived the coastal wind and salt air.

SOLUTION

Makeover enhances the tranquil view and removes the separation between outside and in.

Carefully selected plants thrive in the wind and salt-laden air.

Bird's-eye View

THIS BALCONY was just a narrow landing outside a condominium's back door until the resident turned it into a bright and lively landscape of flowers. Most of the railing now disappears in a sweep of blooms in window boxes, which stretch for 8 feet along the rail. Looking out the window from his home office, the gardener sees his plantings in the foreground;

BEFORE

when he stands on the balcony, the flowers are at his fingertips. Under the window, blossoms in a narrow planter mirror the colors in the window boxes. Glazed pots of perennials are tucked into the corners of the balcony, leaving ample room to come up the stairs with an armload of groceries.

The annuals are planted twice a year—once in spring, then again in summer or fall—so the colorful ribbon of blooms always looks fresh and in tune with the season. Including plants with colored foliage makes the scene even brighter.

CHALLENGE

The corridor balcony is a shared walkway between condominiums, so it has to stay open.

The hot balcony looked faded and colorless.

SOLUTION

Small pots and a narrow box of upright plants under the window leave the walkway clear.

Hanging blue boxes filled with colorful, trailing flowers and foliage brighten the railing.

PLANT HIGHLIGHTS

Dwarf lily-of-the-Nile
Agapanthus 'Peter Pan'

Heuchera 'Santa Ana Cardinal'

Million bells
Calibrachoa

Purple-leaf basil
Ocimum basilicum

Spider flower
Cleome hasslerana

Verbena hybrids

The Sky's the Limit

GREAT BIG GLAZED POTS were the main thing this gardener needed to turn a bare, sunny rooftop into a lush garden. The bright Oriental pots were filled with lightweight potting soil and planted with small trees, shrubs, and annual and perennial flowers— just like an in-ground garden. The owner had a water line and a spigot installed on the roof.

BEFORE

Even though this is a substantial garden room (15 by 25 feet), the richness of the plantings makes it seem even bigger. There's plenty of space for a table and chairs and a market umbrella among the flowers; the view of neighboring rooftops and trees adds to the comfortable and airy ambience. Repeated elements, like the trailing ivy geranium planted at the bases of shrubs, give the garden continuity.

Primary colors keep the mood playful. A glazed pot was used as a table base; it's topped with a surface just large enough for drinks and snacks. The big red umbrella and shiny spheres brighten the scene.

PLANT HIGHLIGHTS

Crape myrtle
Lagerstroemia indica

Golden marguerite
Anthemis tinctoria

Scotch heather
Calluna vulgaris

Snapdragon
Antirrhinum majus

Transvaal daisy
Gerbera jamesonii

122

Owners wanted an intimate setting without losing the balcony's open feel.

There were no planting beds where a garden might grow.

Cheery colors, clustered plants, and shaded table and chairs make a cozy patio in one corner of the space.

Tiered container plantings emulate garden beds.

Comfort
Zones

Hidden Assets

A stone wall and a strategically placed tree provide all the privacy needed for this front yard retreat. The tree screens the table and chairs from the street, and a market umbrella offers shelter from the sun and completes the feeling of enclosure. The palette is simple, sophisticated, and natural.

Open Seating

LEFT: **When the owners of this garden relax on their patio, they're surrounded by the color and drama of ornamental grasses. The dense planting and surrounding trees protect the gravel patio from the wind.**

Grape Shape

Grapevines cling to their arbor supports, creating a cool place to sit and enjoy the view. The gnarled vines look sculptural through the winter, and the large leaves provide cool shade all summer long. When the fruit is ripe, no decoration could be more beautiful.

In Ruins

A pair of antique doors inspired a 21st-century family to revive 18th-century garden fashion and build their own back-yard ruin. The fine old doors are flanked by new columns set into what seems to be a crumbling façade. A reflecting pond edged in handsome stone completes the garden retreat.

Points to Ponder

RIGHT: Moisture-loving plants flourish in the tops of hollow stone columns that rise dramatically from the middle of a pond. The columns' broad capitals hold enough soil for the plants; copper tubing brings water up to them through the columns. As the water overflows, it trickles gently back into the pond.

Rock Walk

BELOW: Smooth stones set in a thick green lawn lead across this quiet garden. Right in the middle of the path, a large, lichen-encrusted stone is set slightly above grade, creating a subtle focal point in the peaceful, grassy expanse.

Sun Spot

BELOW: Where there isn't enough room for a pond or a fountain, a simple reflecting pool can add a note of serene grace. This stone basin, set among low-growing greenery, captures the light and invites birds in for a bath or a drink.

A Perfect Moment

ABOVE: Summer flowers spill across the wonderful pebble mosaic
of this patio floor. The smooth stones are laid in a swirling pattern
as intricate as the design of an Oriental carpet. No wonder the
gardener set up a daybed outdoors.

Room in a View

RIGHT: A terrace patio under the enormous, spreading branches of
an old oak is simply and perfectly furnished with a pair of graceful
wicker chairs and an antique table. The tile floor heightens the
beauty of the open yet intimate outdoor room.

A Touch of Red

RIGHT: The sweeping curves of a pagoda-style roof cast a romantic spell over this garden bridge. As you approach, bright red elliptical arches under the roof redefine the space, drawing your eye into the sheltered area in the middle of the bridge.

Day Glow

BELOW: This fancy Victorian wrought-iron bench might never have been painted in bright colors in its own day—but it looks just right in brilliant blue, glowing among the complementary hues of a perennial garden in full bloom.

Snapshot
Solutions

IN A WEEKEND

Wooden Bridge

Even the simplest bridge lets you admire
your garden from a new perspective. Here,
smoothly rounded river rocks and graceful
bog and water plants both soften and define
the edges of a low wood-plank bridge.

Bridges mark a transition in the garden, creating a sense of anticipation even before you take the first step across. They look most natural spanning a pond, but they can also cross ditches or any dip in the terrain sharp enough to suggest a short leap. Adults like to linger on a bridge, enjoying the changing views of the garden as they stroll over. Children love the fun and fantasy of running across, even if it's only over the treacherous waters of a lily pond.

To take advantage of the enjoyment generated by even the simplest plank bridge, set it off with dramatic plantings like those shown here.

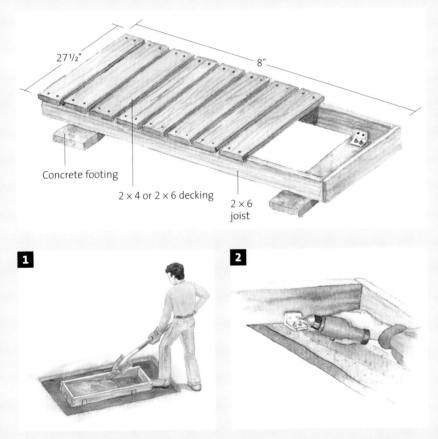

27½"

8"

Concrete footing

2 × 4 or 2 × 6 decking

2 × 6 joist

1

2

STEP ONE: **Prepare the footings at each end of the bridge by digging two 3-inch-deep, about 2- by 4-foot holes. In the holes, build forms out of 2 by 4s; the forms should measure 1 by 3 feet. Check that the tops of the forms are level. Drive stakes into the soil on the outside of the forms and fasten them to the forms with nails. Mix concrete and shovel it into the forms; smooth the top with a screed board. (See photograph on page 13.)**

STEP TWO: **While the concrete is still wet, cut the joists and rim joists to size and nail them together. Set the joist assembly in place on top of the concrete forms. Temporarily set the brackets against the inside of each joist, centered in the footing. Mark placement of bolts. Remove the brackets and embed the bolts in the concrete with about 1 inch of the threaded end exposed. Place the brackets on the bolts and fasten with nuts. Once the concrete has hardened, remove the wood forms and attach the joists to the brackets with screws.**

STEP THREE: **Cut decking boards long enough to overhang the joists by 1 inch on each side (see illustration above left). Attach the decking with screws driven into joists. To help keep the lumber from rotting, space the boards about ¼ inch apart; this allows water and debris to fall through. (Use a piece of wood for a spacer as you go along.) If desired, coat the bridge with a suitable exterior finish; recoat it every year or two.**

MATERIALS & TOOLS Two 2 by 4s, 8 feet long, for forms • 12 wooden stakes, about 1 foot long • Two 2 by 6s, 8 feet long, plus one 2 by 6, 4 feet long, for joists • 2 by 4 or 2 by 6 decking boards • 2 bags ready-to-use concrete mix • Screed board, 3 feet long • 4 galvanized right-angle brackets with foundation anchor bolts, nuts, and screws • Screws for decking • Nails • Carpenter's level • Electric drill and screwdriving bits

STEP ONE: Pour potting mix into a bucket and moisten it.

STEP TWO: Mix in controlled-release fertilizer in the amount directed on the package. Place enough mix in the pot so that the top of the anchor plant's root ball will rest about 2 inches below the pot rim; then tamp the mix lightly to firm it.

STEP THREE: Arrange plants, still in their nursery containers, inside the big pot; move them around until you're pleased with the design, then remove them from the pot. Knock the anchor plant from its nursery container, rough up its root ball with your fingers, and center it in the big pot.

STEP FOUR: Add more potting mix. Set in smaller flowering and foliage plants, positioning them so the tops of their root balls are about 2 inches below the pot rim. Tuck any trailing plants near the edges of the pot. Firm the potting mix around all root balls and water the planted pot thoroughly.

QUICK IDEA

A lavishly planted big pot guarantees quick
excitement and drama, whether you display it on your deck or patio or set it right in a garden bed. Put the pot in its permanent location before planting, since it will be heavy once filled with soil. When choosing plants, start with an anchor plant such as a small shrub for the pot's center; then fill in around it with colorful annuals and perennials.

MATERIALS & TOOLS Large pot • Potting mix • Controlled-release fertilizer • Plants, including a small shrub for the center of the pot and smaller flowering and foliage plants • Bucket

STEP ONE: For the sides of the box, cut each 4 by 6 in half to make twelve 4-foot-long pieces. Cut the 2 by 2 into eight pieces, each 1½ feet long. To make the caps for the box, cut both 2 by 6s in half, making the cuts at a 45° angle. Then cut off the square ends of the resulting four 2 by 6 pieces at a 45° angle.

STEP TWO: Stack the 4 by 6s with joints overlapping, as shown in illustration at right. To hold the box together, attach the 1½-foot-long pieces of 2 by 2 to each interior corner and the middle of each side, using wood screws. Lay the 2 by 6 cap pieces in place, with their inner edges even with the inner edges of the box. Attach the 2 by 2s to the caps with wood screws. To reinforce the cap, screw the cap boards to the 4 by 6s below.

STEP THREE: Install the box in a level spot. If desired, use landscape fabric to cover the ground under the box. Fill with good, fast-draining soil; then set in plants.

DO IT TODAY

A raised-box planter is the perfect place for herbs, small-growing summer vegetables, or flowers for cutting. You can fill the box with good, fast-draining soil (rather than struggling with poor native soil in the garden), and the 20-inch height makes it easy to harvest crops without stooping. We give directions for building one box, but you can easily extend your garden by assembling more boxes.

MATERIALS & TOOLS 6 redwood 4 by 6s, 8 feet long • 1 redwood 2 by 2, 8 feet long • 2 redwood 2 by 6s, 8 feet long • Good, fast-draining soil • Wood screws • Landscape fabric (optional) • Power saw

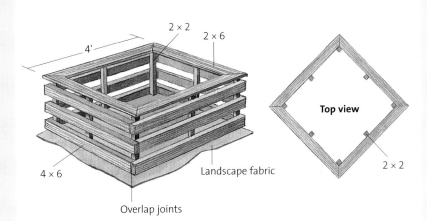

133

Instant Pond

Softly swaying ornamental grasses, including (left to right) reddish pheasant's-tail grass, blue oat grass, and Mexican feather grass, make a dramatic backdrop for this small pond. Pink-flowered thrift and sedum grow in front.

Much of the work is already done for you when you buy a rigid, pre-formed pond liner. These liners come in various sizes, shapes, and depths; shelves for plants are built right in. All you have to do is dig a hole large enough for the liner, edge it with your favorite stone, and choose the plants.

The owner of this pond installed a solar-powered pump and fountain, so he didn't have to worry about an electrical outlet. Weathered flag-stones hide the plastic lip of the liner. The stones look perfectly natural among the ornamental grasses and tufts of spreading, mossy-looking plants that grow around the pool.

1

2

STEP ONE: Select a flat, open area with plenty of sunshine. Remove sod and any plants. Set the pond liner, right side up, in place; mark its outline in the soil with a yardstick. Set the liner aside and make a more visible outline with sand.

STEP TWO: Begin by digging a hole 2 inches wider than the liner and 2 inches deeper than the depth of the shelves (the extra 2 inches provide room for a cushioning layer of sand). Set the liner in the hole; mark the areas where you will have to dig deeper to accommodate the rest of the liner. Finish digging the hole, again making it 2 inches deeper than the liner. Remove any roots and stones from the bottom of the hole; use a carpenter's level to make sure it is flat. Add 2 inches of sand and set the liner in the hole.

STEP THREE: Make sure the top edge of the liner is level; remove liner and make any adjustments. Start filling the liner with a slow trickle of water. At the same time, begin backfilling by placing a 4-inch layer of sand around the outside of the liner. Tamp sand down around liner with a short length of wood or a trowel handle. Add and tamp more layers of sand to fill space around liner completely; press more sand under rim of pond to support it. Add mosquito-control ring (see page 16).

STEP FOUR: Edge pond with stones to hide liner's rim. Make sure most of each stone's weight rests on soil. Set solar panel for fountain nearby in a sunny, south-facing spot; place pump in pond.

MATERIALS & TOOLS Rigid pond liner • Sand • Edging stones • Solar pump and fountain • Carpenter's level • Mosquito-control ring

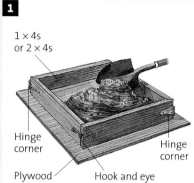

1 × 4s
or 2 × 4s

Hinge
corner

Hinge
corner

Plywood

Hook and eye

STEP ONE: **Make a form of the desired size using 1 by 2 or 2 by 4 lumber. Use screws to fasten one corner; then, for ease in unmolding, hinge two of the remaining corners and fasten final corner with a hook and eye. Set the prepared form on a piece of plywood. Apply a mold release agent or vegetable oil to all surfaces that will come in contact with the concrete.**

DO IT TODAY
—————

Concrete stepping-stones you make yourself

give your walkways a distinctive, personal character. Decorate each stone with impressions of large, firm-textured leaves; or use fern fronds to achieve a fossil-like look. Or invite children to press their hands or feet into the damp concrete. If you need a number of stepping-stones, you can speed up production by constructing several forms.

STEP TWO: **Mix concrete, shovel it into the form, and tamp it into the corners. Then level the concrete with a screed board (see photo 2, page 13). Draw a concrete edging tool along the edges of the form; this bevels the edges of the stepping-stone, making it less likely to chip. Smooth the surface with finishing trowel.**

STEP THREE: **Allow concrete to firm up for a few minutes. Press leaves into the concrete so they make a clear impression; then peel them off. Let concrete set for a few hours; then remove mold. Let concrete cure for several days; spray lightly with water each day. If desired, use wood stain or latex paint to highlight the leaf patterns.**

MATERIALS & TOOLS 1 by 2 or 2 by 4 lumber for the form • Plywood for the bottom of the form • Fast-setting concrete mix • Screed board, at least 1 foot longer than diameter of stepping-stone • Mold release agent (form oil) or vegetable oil • Wood screws • Hinges • Hook and eye • Concrete edging or joint tool • Concrete finishing trowel • Firm-textured leaves • Wood stain or latex paint (optional)

motion, rub the grout firmly into the gaps between the tile pieces.

STEP THREE: Let grout set for 10 to 15 minutes. Barely moisten cloth scraps; rub them firmly over surface of mosaic to compact the grout further and remove excess grout. After grout has hardened, polish the surface with a clean cloth scrap. Remove masking tape. Let grout cure, following the label instructions.

MATERIALS & TOOLS New terra-cotta pot • Masking tape • Glazed tiles • Foam brush • Mosaic adhesive • Premixed tile grout • Latex or plastic gloves • Lint-free cloth scraps • Hammer • Bucket

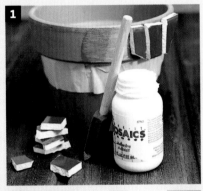

QUICK IDEA

Pots in mosaic style

bring a bright flair to a plain terra-cotta container. The pots shown here are decorated with inexpensive tiles purchased at a home improvement store, but you might also use bits of pottery, glass, stained glass, or mirrors. Or try marbles, flat pebbles, or even metallic objects such as buttons or pieces of costume jewelry. If you decide to mix materials, be sure to select pieces of similar thickness.

STEP ONE: Fasten a strip of masking tape under the pot's lip so the edge will be clean after gluing and grouting. Place the tiles between several sheets of newspaper and tap them with a hammer to break them into pieces.

Wearing gloves, use the foam brush to apply a thin layer of mosaic adhesive around the pot's lip. Apply more adhesive to the back of each piece of tile, taking care to cover the entire surface. Affix tile pieces to the pot's lip, spacing them 1/8 to 1/4 inch apart. Let the adhesive dry for at least 12 hours.

STEP TWO: Wearing gloves, scoop out a small handful of grout and press it onto the surface of the mosaic. With a circular

Large patios take a good bit of time and effort to build—but this small, detached brick circle is another story. It can easily be installed in a couple of days, and it doesn't require truckloads of materials. Tuck it into a corner of your garden to create a peaceful private retreat.

STEP ONE: **Rototill or dig soil, removing sod and roots; rake it smooth. (In areas where soil freezes, you may need to excavate several inches of soil and spread a layer of gravel to help prevent frost heaving; consult your local building department.) Place a stake in soil to mark the patio's center; tie a length of string to it. Then tie other end of the string to the second stake so that you have 3 ½ feet of string between the two stakes. With free stake, trace the patio's outline in the soil, pulling string taut as you walk in a circle around center stake. Remove stakes and mark the outline with powdered limestone or gypsum. Lay the 2 by 4 across the circle; place the carpenter's level on it to make sure soil is level. Recheck level at every stage.**

STEP TWO: **Pour six bags of sand evenly over the soil to about 5 inches beyond the edge of the outline. Smooth sand with one edge of the 2 by 4, then tamp to make it firm and even. Spray with a fine mist from the hose; tamp again to make a layer 2 inches thick.**

Number of bricks per row

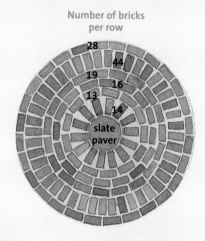

28
44
19
16
13
14
slate paver

STEP THREE: **Place the round paver in the middle of the sand circle. Working from the center outward, set down bricks, as shown below left; tap them into place with the mallet and butt them together tightly. Spread three bags of sand evenly over surface of finished paving. If sand is damp, let it dry; then sweep it into joints between bricks. Mist lightly. Keep on adding sand until the joints are full.**

STEP FOUR: **To mortar the center paver and adjacent bricks in place (optional, but recommended), mix mortar; add color, if desired. Using a brick trowel (or a grout bag), apply mortar between bricks immediately surrounding center paver. Let mortar dry; wipe away excess with a clean rag.**

STEP FIVE: **Pour the remaining sand around the patio's perimeter, mist it with the hose, and pack it firmly. To help reinforce the patio's edge, lay sod or plant low ground covers close to it.**

MATERIALS & TOOLS One 2 by 4, 7 feet long • 2 stakes, 1 foot long • Powdered limestone or gypsum • 12 bags sand (1 cubic foot each; about ½ cubic yard total) • 1 round slate or flagstone paver, about 17 inches in diameter • 150 used bricks (includes a few extras for color matching) • String • Rotary tiller or spade • Tamper • Carpenter's level • Rubber mallet • 1 bag mortar mix (80 pounds), optional • 1 quart mortar color (optional) • Grout bag (optional) • Brick trowel (optional)

Instant Patio

Decorated with a small bistro table and chairs, this little patio is a favored garden destination. Brightly blooming annuals and perennials such as yellow sunflowers, golden coreopsis, and purple coneflowers enhance the cozy setting.

Wall fountains enliven courtyards, side yards, and other small spaces where you'd like to enjoy the refreshing sound of water without crowding a path or a limited seating area. In this courtyard garden, a wisteria vine and ferny foliage plants thrive in the dappled light around a cool, gently splashing fountain. The brick wall makes a distinguished backdrop for the terra-cotta sunburst.

The best wall fountains seem to spout water as if from a hidden spring. A simple lattice (or vines and other plantings) will conceal the tubing that carries water to the fountain.

STEP ONE: **Place the mask face down on a soft surface. Glue corks to the back of the mask to lift it far enough away from the wall to allow the tubing to run behind it. With a masonry bit, drill a hole for the metal dowel at a 45° angle halfway through the mask, a few inches above the waterspout hole. Also drill about a 1½-inch-deep hole at a 45° angle into the wall where you'll hang the mask.**

STEP TWO: **Cut a piece of vinyl tubing long enough to wind down the wall behind the vines or latticework trellis to reach the basin. Slide the elbow fitting into one end of the tubing. Cut a second piece of tubing, connect it to the other end of the fitting, and push it through the back of the mask's waterspout hole.**

STEP THREE: **Push the metal dowel into the hole in the wall. Hang the mask on the wall by sliding it over the protruding half of the dowel.**

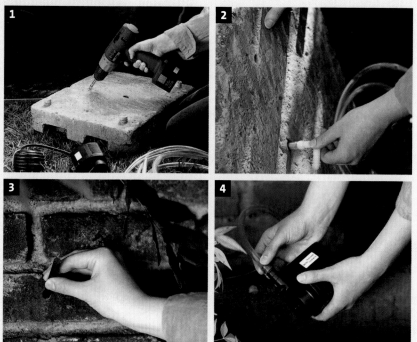

STEP FOUR: **With mask in place, lead the tubing down the wall, concealing it behind vines or lattice. Slide the other end of the tubing over pump outlet; place the pump in the basin. Fill the basin with water. Plug the pump into a grounded outlet.**

MATERIALS & TOOLS Mask with waterspout hole • Corks • Clear vinyl tubing • Elbow fitting for vinyl tubing • Metal dowel, about 3 inches long • Small submersible pump • Watertight basin • Electric drill and masonry bit • Waterproof glue

STEP ONE: **To make a watering tube, cut a piece of PVC pipe so one end will be even with the jar's rim when the pipe is set upright in the jar. Cap the pipe on one end. Drill ⅛-inch-diameter holes about 1 inch apart all around the pipe.**

STEP TWO: **Pour potting mix into a bucket and moisten it; mix in controlled-release fertilizer in the amount directed on the package. Partially fill the jar with potting mix; then insert the watering tube, capped end down, near the center, taking care not to block the jar's drainage hole. Add more potting mix, loosely filling the jar to the rim.**

STEP THREE: **Working from the bottom up, plant pockets, pushing roots firmly into jar; add potting mix around roots as needed. Plant the top of the jar. Water well.**

STEP FOUR: **To irrigate plants, slip a funnel into the PVC pipe and pour water into it; the holes drilled in the pipe will distribute water evenly. Feed monthly with liquid fertilizer.**

MATERIALS & TOOLS Strawberry jar, at least 16 inches tall • PVC pipe • Cap for pipe • Potting mix • Controlled-release fertilizer • Liquid fertilizer • Strawberry plants • Funnel • Electric drill • Bucket

QUICK IDEA

A strawberry jar provides a harvest of sweet fruit in a small space. Or, if you prefer, fill your pocketed jar with sun-loving herbs, interesting succulents, or a variety of bright annual flowers. Always use a big jar (at least 16 inches tall), since smaller ones dry out too quickly. Also look for one with generously flared, cup-shaped pockets; these hold moisture better than very narrow, slitlike pockets do.

IN A WEEKEND

Stone Wall

A low stacked stone wall gives structure to a hillside garden and looks handsome throughout the year. Here, a bright mix of cosmos, bachelor's buttons, and zinnias offers a bounty of cut flowers for summer bouquets.

This stone wall fits naturally into a gentle slope, providing a handsome, enduring boundary for beds filled with trees, shrubs, perennials, and ground covers. Since the stones are laid without mortar, you can rearrange them as you work, changing their positions to create the most pleasing pattern. Keep in mind, though, that large stones like these are heavy; having a helper will move the project along more quickly and easily.

STEP ONE: **Lay out the location of your wall, using hose or string to mark the outline. Then mark the outline again (just inside the hose or string) with powdered limestone or gypsum or by digging a line in the soil with a shovel; remove hose or string. Measure the length of the wall and decide on its height, keeping in mind that you should limit the height to 3 feet or less (a taller wall will need a concrete footing). Order the stones.**

Construct a footing. For a 2- to 3-foot-high wall, dig a 6- to 8-inch-deep trench, making it level on the bottom and a bit wider than your largest stones. Tamp the soil in the trench to firm it. Set aside some of the flattest and best-looking stones for the wall's top layer. Then select large, flat stones, each about the same size, to give the wall a sturdy base. Place one layer of stones in the trench, fitting them together.

STEP TWO: **Add the next layer, staggering the stones so that the joints are not on top of each other. Backfill with soil as each layer is added. Lightly tamp the soil each time you backfill to reduce settling. As you stack the stones, keep in mind that the wall should lean back into the slope approximately 1 inch for every foot of height to provide stability. Check periodically with a carpenter's level to make sure the wall is fairly level along its length. Make adjustments as you work, trying out stones of various sizes to help keep the wall level and filling in gaps with small stones.**

STEP THREE: **Set the top layer of stones in place. Check for level. Backfill behind the finished wall and tamp the soil, taking care not to compact it too much (this could put undue stress on the finished wall).**

MATERIALS & TOOLS Flat stones • Hose or string • Powdered limestone or gypsum (optional) • Tamper • Carpenter's level

DO IT TODAY

A flagstone and gravel path gives the

garden structure and offers clean, easy access to the beds—no matter how wet the weather. Made from irregularly shaped flagstones set off by small pebbles chosen for their complementary colors, the pathway has the look of a mosaic. To create a soft edging, line both sides of the walk with border plants such as blue fescue and petunias.

STEP ONE: Mark the outline of the path with powdered limestone or gypsum. Excavate the soil to a depth of 4 inches. Tamp soil to make it firm. Install benderboard edging as described in Step 1, page 79. Place landscape fabric over the path to suppress weeds, tucking it firmly under the edges of the benderboard.

STEP TWO: Pour a 2-inch-thick layer of sand over the landscape fabric and rake it smooth. As you rake, moisten the sand with a fine spray from the hose. Tamp the moist sand to make it firm and level. Arrange the flagstones on the sand, wiggling them into the sand so they are firmly embedded. Use a carpenter's level on a long board to check for level; add or remove sand as needed to make the path level and adjust the height of the stones.

STEP THREE: Finish the path by filling the cracks between the stones with gravel.

MATERIALS & TOOLS Powdered limestone or gypsum • Lengths of benderboard, 8 feet long by 4 inches wide • 1 by 2 stakes, 1 foot long • Wood screws • Landscape fabric • Coarse or builder's sand • Flagstones (1 to 2 inches thick) • Decorative gravel • Tamper • Carpenter's level

STEP ONE: Paint the 8-inch pots burnt orange; let them dry for a few minutes. Paint the rims of the pots straw yellow. Let dry for 10 to 15 minutes.

STEP TWO: Pour potting mix into a bucket and moisten it. Mix in controlled-release fertilizer in the amount directed on the package. Fill the painted pots with moistened potting mix. Set one purple kale plant in the center of each pot; around it, alternate pansies with three or four dusty miller plants. Water well.

STEP THREE: Set the planter box in its permanent location (it will be quite heavy when full). Partially fill it with potting mix. Invert the 5-inch pots; space the upended pots evenly in the box, so that their bottoms are just below the rim of the box. Fill in around them with potting mix, leaving the bottoms uncovered. Set the green-and-white kale plants at the ends of the box. Along its sides, alternate pansies and dusty miller. Place two pansies between each inverted 5-inch pot. Water well.

STEP FOUR: Set the planted 8-inch pots on top of the inverted pots.

QUICK IDEA

A two-tiered planter box brimming with

festive flowers is a charming way to welcome each change of seasons. Greet spring with tulips and primroses; in summer, showcase a mixed bouquet of coreopsis, nasturtiums, and geraniums. When cool fall days arrive, fill the planter with cheerful pansies and striking foliage plants, as shown here. At any time of year, choose plants that complement the pretty painted pots.

MATERIALS & TOOLS 3 terra-cotta pots, 8 inches in diameter • 3 terra-cotta azalea pots (short, wide pots), 5 inches in diameter • Green wooden planter box, about 3 feet long, 10 inches wide, and 10½ inches tall • 1 bag potting mix (2 cubic feet) • Controlled-release fertilizer • 3 purple ornamental kale plants in 4-inch pots • 4 green-and-white ornamental kale plants in 4-inch pots • 2 six-packs purple pansies • 2 six-packs orange pansies • 4 six-packs 'Trick or Treat' pansies (orange with black face) • 3 six-packs dusty miller • 1 pint acrylic burnt orange paint • 1 pint acrylic straw yellow paint • Foam brush • Bucket

Gazebo Express

Fast-growing vines such as star jasmine climb up the wooden arbors of the free-form gazebo, covering it with sweetly fragrant flowers. A blooming border encircles the graceful structure.

This quick-to-construct gazebo, with walls made of prefabricated arbors and an umbrella for a roof, goes together in less than a day, giving you an intimate setting for alfresco meals or quiet conversations. Set it amid a wide, lush border and surround it with flowers; or, for more drama, place it in the middle of the lawn. Train flowering vines up and over the arbors to decorate and screen your new garden room.

STEP ONE: Assemble the arbors, if necessary. Paint them, if you wish.

STEP TWO: Select a level site. Rototill or dig the soil and rake it smooth and level. Place a stake in the soil to mark the center of the gazebo; tie a length of string to it. Then tie the other end of the string to the second stake so that you have 4½ feet of string between the two stakes. With the free stake, trace the outline for the benderboard border in the soil, pulling the string taut as you walk in a circle around the center stake. Remove the stakes and mark the outline with powdered limestone or gypsum.

STEP THREE: Decide where the main entry to the gazebo will be (from a lawn or path, for example) and lay out the location for the arbors as if they were the four main points of a compass. The front legs of each should be just outside the edge of the marked circle.

STEP FOUR: Open the umbrella to determine the height of its outer rim. The legs of each arbor will be set in gravel-filled holes to make their peaks even with or a few inches lower than the rim of the umbrella. (Here, the final height of each arbor is 7 feet.) Dig holes for the arbor legs, place gravel in the holes, and insert the legs. Use a carpenter's level to check that each arbor's sides and front are vertical before filling the holes.

STEP FIVE: Lay out the benderboard border. Using 1½-inch screws, fasten benderboard pieces to the front legs of each arbor, with the top edge of the benderboard about 1 inch above ground level; these edges will form a low retaining wall for the decomposed granite. Overlap sections of benderboard by about 4 inches, screwing them together with ⅝-inch screws.

STEP SIX: For added strength, tamp more gravel around the arbor legs. Spread decomposed granite in the center area, dampen it lightly, and compact it with a tamper.

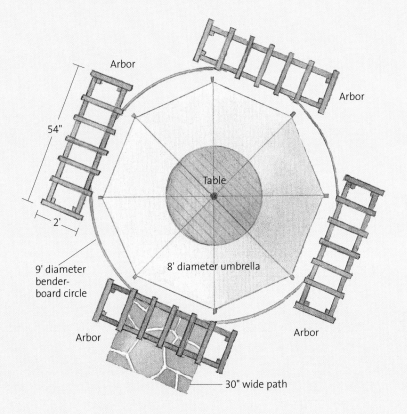

MATERIALS & TOOLS 4 garden arbors, approximately 8 feet high, 2 feet deep, and 4½ feet wide • Paint (optional) • Outdoor umbrella, approximately 8 feet in diameter • Table to fit under umbrella • 2 stakes, 1 foot long • Gravel • ½ cubic yard decomposed granite • 4 lengths of benderboard, 8 feet long by 4 inches wide • Powdered limestone or gypsum • String • 1½-inch screws • ⅝-inch screws • Rotary tiller or spade • Tamper • Carpenter's level

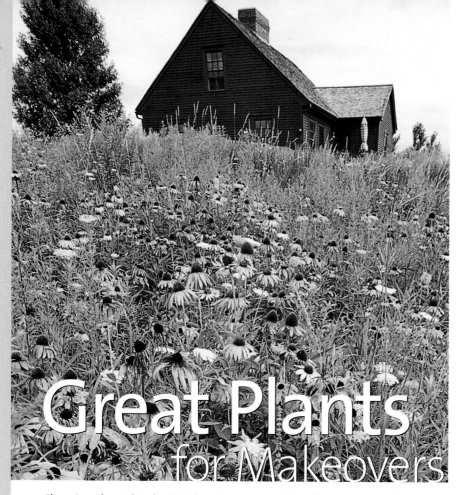

Great Plants
for Makeovers

Choosing the right plants is key to a successful makeover. Select plants from these 10 lists to change your garden from bland to grand.

Meadow Makers

Convert a lawn into a meadow with a carefree mix of grasses and wildflowers.

Butterfly weed
Asclepias tuberosa

Growing to 3 ft. high, this clumping perennial sports clusters of bright flowers in shades of orange, yellow, and red. Butterflies are attracted to the flowers, which are also great for cutting. Blooms summer to autumn. Quite cold hardy (to −30°F). Full sun. Moderate water.

Coreopsis

Easy-to-grow sunflower relatives. Annual *Coreopsis tinctoria* blooms summer through fall in yellows, oranges, and reds. Perennials *C. grandiflora* and *C. lanceolata* form leafy mounds topped by bright yellow summer flowers. *C. verticillata* 'Moonbeam' produces clouds of pale yellow blooms. All are hardy to −30°F. Full sun. Little to moderate water.

Cornflower
Centaurea cyanus

From spring through midsummer, this carefree annual blooms in shades of blue, pink, rose, or white atop plants reaching 1½ ft. tall. Often reseeds. Polka Dot strain has flowers in full range of colors. Full sun. Moderate water.

Daylily
Hemerocallis

Tough and adaptable perennials that look great in casual drifts. Arching, sword-shaped leaves are topped in spring or summer by lilylike flowers in a wide range of colors. Deciduous (hardy to −40°F) and evergreen types (better for temperate climates) are available. Full sun or partial shade. Regular water.

Fescue
Festuca

These perennial grasses form low clumps or tufts, some with interesting flower spikes in late spring or summer. Common blue fescue (*F. glauca*), hardy to −30°F, makes a great silvery blue accent. Red fescue (*F. rubra*) is even more cold tolerant. Full sun or partial shade. Moderate to regular water.

Grama grass
Bouteloua

Perennial grasses that stand 1–2 ft. tall with dark red to purple flower spikes dangling attractively on upright wiry stems. Native to North America, they take heat in stride and survive to −20°F. Full sun. Little water.

Poppy
Papaver

Hard to beat for spring and summer color. Foot-tall Iceland poppy (*P. nudicaule*) produces large fragrant flowers in yellow, orange, pink, and white. It is supremely cold tolerant. Flanders field poppy (*P. rhoeas*), an annual growing to 3 ft. tall, offers blooms in a wide range of colors and does best in cool-summer areas. Full sun. Moderate to regular water.

Sedge
Carex

Grasslike perennials grown for their arching leaves, often striped or oddly colored. Favorites include blonde sedge (*C. albula*), with silvery green leaves; leather leaf sedge (*C. buchananii*), with curly-tipped, reddish bronze foliage; and blue sedge (*C. flacca*), which can be clipped like a lawn. Hardiness and water and exposure needs vary with type.

Yarrow
Achillea

These carefree perennials bloom in a wide range of colors in summer and early fall. Flowers usually in flattish clusters. Fragrant foliage forms attractive clumps or mats. Hardiness varies with type. Full sun. Little to moderate water.

Green Screens

Block noise or unsightly views and create discrete garden "rooms" with these versatile evergreen plants.

Bamboo

Diverse group of fast-growing grasses, many in the 6- to 15-ft. range. Use deep, in-ground barriers to contain running types; clumping types can be used like garden shrubs. Many can be grown in containers and moved to a protected area in winter. Among the hardiest are species of *Fargesia* (clumping) and *Phyllostachys* (running). Full sun or partial shade. Moderate to regular water.

Boxwood
Buxus

Small to medium-size billowy shrubs. Dense cover of small, uniform leaves makes them great for clipping into formal shapes. Korean

OTHER GREAT CHOICES

Arborvitae *Thuja*

Myrica

Myrtle *Myrtus communis*

Sweet olive *Osmanthus fragrans*

Viburnum (several)

Yew *Taxus*

boxwood *(B. microphylla koreana)* grows to 2½ ft. and is hardy to −20°F. A good choice for warmer areas is Japanese boxwood *(B. m. japonica)*, which can reach 6 ft. tall if left unpruned. Sun or shade. Regular water.

Glossy abelia
Abelia × grandiflora

Graceful shrub with arching branches covered in small, glossy leaves and white to pale pink flowers. Grows to 8 ft. tall and 5 ft. wide, making it ideal for a medium-height screen. Smaller varieties are available. Hardy to 0°F. Full sun or partial shade. Regular water.

Heavenly bamboo
Nandina domestica

Delicate-looking but adaptable 6- to 8-ft. shrub for temperate regions (stems damaged at 5°F). Canes and lacy foliage are reminiscent of bamboo, but leaves emerge pink and red, mature to soft green, and in fall take on purple and bronze tints. White flowers and red berries enhance the colorful display. Sun or shade. Little to regular water.

Holly
Ilex

Many types available in a wide range of sizes, most with glossy, spiny leaves and colorful berries. English holly *(I. aquifolium)* and Chinese holly *(I. cornuta)* are good choices for temperate regions; Japanese holly *(I. crenata)* and *I. × meserveae* survive temperatures of −10°F. Full sun or partial shade. Regular water.

Japanese privet
Ligustrum japonicum

Dense, compact growth to 12 ft. tall, but can be kept lower by pruning. Abundant white flowers have distinctive fragrance; their numbers are reduced on frequently clipped plants. Several varieties available, some with foliage attractively variegated with gray or creamy white. Hardy to 0°F. Full sun or partial shade. Regular water.

Pittosporum

Great for warmer regions, especially in coastal gardens. Most have glossy leaves and tiny, fragrant flowers. Even unclipped, plants have attractive form. *P. crassifolium* and *P. tobira* make excellent 10- to 15-ft. hedges or windbreaks. Fallen fruit is sticky; plants best placed away from sidewalks and lawns. Full sun or partial shade. Moderate to regular water.

Podocarpus

Handsome foliage and interesting form make these first-rate screening and background plants for areas where temperatures stay above zero. Most are easily pruned to desired shape and size. Fern pine *(P. gracilior)* and shrubby yew pine *(P. macrophyllus maki)* are two of the best. Full sun or partial shade. Regular water.

Prunus

Evergreen types make attractive, tall privacy screens. Carolina laurel cherry *(P. caroliniana)* and hollyleaf cherry *(P. ilicifolia)* can be kept clipped to a height of 20 ft. English laurel *(P. laurocerasus)* grows quickly to 15–30 ft. tall, and several shorter varieties (wider than tall) are available. Hardiness varies with type. Full sun. Moderate to regular water.

Between the Lines

Use these low-growing plants to create a niche garden among stones—or replace boring mulch or bare soil with a fragrant or flowering carpet.

Baby's tears
Soleirolia soleirolii*

Tiny leaves form a lush green carpet 1–4 in. tall. Grows quickly in moist places and covers difficult, shady areas well. Recovers from occasional foot traffic. Plant where temperatures stay above 32°F. Partial shade. Regular water.

Blue star creeper
Pratia pedunculata*

Charming star-shaped, pale blue flowers dot this creeping mat of green. When not in bloom, it resembles baby's tears (see above) but survives temperatures of −20°F and can take a bit more foot traffic. Full sun or partial shade. Regular water.

Carpet bugle
Ajuga reptans*

Forms a 4-in.-tall spreading mass of dark green, bronze-tinted, or colorfully variegated leaves. Blue, pink, or white flower spikes grow to 6 in. tall in spring and early summer. Hardy to −40°F. Full sun or partial shade. Regular water.

Chamomile
Chamaemelum nobile

Soft fernlike leaves form spreading bright green clumps 3–12 in. high. Flowers resemble tiny daisies or yellow buttons. Plant between stepping-stones or along a path, where passersby can brush past the fragrant leaves. Survives −10°F. Full sun or partial shade. Moderate water.

Irish moss
Sagina subulata*

Forms a bright green, undulating evergreen carpet with the look of moss. Great between stepping-stones or as a small-scale ground cover. Tolerates some foot traffic. Hardy to −30°F. Full sun or partial shade. Regular water.

Mazus reptans

Standing 2 in. tall, this perennial is just right for crevices. Takes heavy foot traffic. Bright green leaves set off the purplish blue flowers in spring and early summer. Hardy to −20°F. Full sun or partial shade. Regular water.

Moss pink
Phlox subulata

A classic choice for rock gardens, this evergreen perennial grows to 6 in. high and is loaded with white, pink, or lavender-blue flowers in late spring or early summer. Hardy to −40°F. Full sun or light shade. Regular water.

Snow-in-summer
Cerastium tomentosum*

Lives up to its name with scores of tiny snow-white blossoms held above silvery gray foliage from late spring into summer. An adaptable and fast-spreading evergreen perennial. Hardy to −40°F. Full sun. Moderate to regular water.

Sweet alyssum
Lobularia maritima*

Honey-scented white, purple, or lavender-pink flowers cover this 2- to 12-in. annual over a long season. Ideal as edging or as a filler among larger plants. Excellent as bulb cover. Full sun. Regular water.

Thyme
Thymus

Spreading evergreen perennials with fragrant foliage. Woolly thyme (*T. pseudolanuginosus*) forms a flat gray-green carpet; may bloom pink in midsummer. Mother-of-thyme (*T. serpyllum*) bears flowers in pink, red, or lavender. Both tolerate light foot traffic. Hardy to −30°F. Full sun or light shade. Moderate water.

*Vigorous spreaders

OTHER GREAT CHOICES
Cranesbill *Erodium*
Golden star *Chrysogonum virginianum*
Gypsophila (low-growing types)
Pussy toes *Antennaria dioica*
Thrift *Armeria maritima*
Woolly yarrow *Achillea tomentosa*

Aerial Artistry

Enliven plain windows, porch or deck railings, and eye-level bare spots with these lush fillers and spillers for hanging baskets, containers, and window boxes.

Bacopa
Sutera cordata

These carefree, low-growing plants reach 2–4 ft. across, depending on variety. Tiny white to lavender-blue flowers appear from spring until frost on trailing branches of aromatic green or gold-splotched leaves. Full sun or partial shade. Regular water.

Begonia

Rhizomatous begonias offer flowers and distinctive foliage that trail over a pot's edge. Semperflorens types, with small, shiny leaves and profuse flowers, make good fillers. Hanging tuberous begonias have large, showy flowers in a wide range of colors. All types thrive in warmth and high humidity. Filtered sun. Regular water.

Coleus
Coleus × hybridus

Leaves with brilliant colors, including chartreuse, yellow, salmon, orange, red, and purple, make these plants the ideal choice for adding a tropical touch. Usually grown as annuals. Choose low-growing types for hanging baskets and containers. Most prefer partial shade; red types take more sun. Regular water.

English ivy
Hedera helix

These sturdy trailers or climbers are classic choices for greening up containers. Look for small-leafed types with interesting leaf shapes—some have ruffled edges, elongated points, or slim lobes. Foliage may be splashed with yellow or white. Full sun or partial shade. Moderate to regular water.

Garden nasturtium
Tropaeolum majus

Easy-to-grow annuals with round, bright green leaves and distinctive flowers in shades of red, yellow, orange, and cream. Look for dwarf varieties, which grow to about 1½ ft. high and wide. Flowers and young leaves add a peppery flavor to salads. Full sun or light shade. Regular water.

Garden verbena
Verbena × hybrida

Sprawling, branching plants reach 3–6 in. high and up to 3 ft. across, depending on variety. Flower colors include white, pink, red, purple, blue, and combinations of these. Snip off spent flowers for waves of repeat bloom. Full sun. Moderate to regular water.

Impatiens walleriana

Popular for brightening shady spots, these tender perennials are usually grown as annuals. They form 1- to 2-ft. mounds of rich green leaves covered in flowers of white, pink, red, orange, or lavender. Partial or full shade. Regular water.

Ipomoea

The lush leaves of these vines look great trailing over containers. Sweet potato (*I. batatas*) leaf colors include pink-and-white variegation, purple-black, and chartreuse. Morning glory (*I. tricolor*) has stunning flowers in many colors. Full sun. Moderate to regular water.

Lobelia erinus

These delicate plants come in compact and trailing forms and offer a profusion of tiny blue flowers from early summer to frost. Compact types reach only 3–6 in. high and 5–9 in. wide; trailing varieties grow to 1½ ft. Partial sun. Regular water.

Million bells
Calibrachoa

Aptly named for their abundant flowers over a long season, these petunia relatives include trailing and clumping types. Available in shades of white, pink, blue, terracotta, or yellow. Full sun or light shade. Regular water.

Patio Partners

Transform a plain patio into a garden room with well-behaved trees and shrubs planted in borders and in colorful containers.

Crape myrtle
*Lagerstroemia indica**

Deciduous tree usually smaller than 25 ft. Showy summer flowers in white, pink, red, or lavender; brilliant fall color. Best in hot-summer regions where winter temperatures remain above zero. Full sun. Moderate water.

Doublefile viburnum
Viburnum plicatum tomentosum

A stunning deciduous shrub. Horizontal branches covered in white spring blooms give a tiered effect. Grows to 10 ft. tall and wider; smaller varieties are available. Hardy to −20°F. Full sun or partial shade. Regular water.

Flowering cherry
Prunus

Graceful small deciduous trees prized for their delicate pink or white spring flowers. Among the best and most popular are *P.* 'Okame', hardy to 0°F, and Taiwan flowering cherry (*P. campanulata*), hardy to 10°F. Full sun. Moderate to regular water.

Flowering maple
*Abutilon**

Flowers in a wide range of colors dangle like bells from arching, leafy branches. Hardy to 20°F, this medium-size evergreen shrub can be grown in containers and moved indoors during cold weather. Full sun or partial shade. Moderate to regular water.

Green hawthorn
Crataegus viridis 'Winter King'

Among the best of the small hawthorns, this variety bears dark green leaves, silvery stems, abundant white flowers, and long-lasting red fruit. Deciduous. Hardy to −20°F. Eventually reaches 25 ft. high and as wide. Full sun. Moderate water.

Japanese aucuba
*Aucuba japonica**

Slow-growing evergreen shrub, ideal for shady spots. It reaches about 10 ft. tall and wide and is offered in variegated forms, with splashes of gold or white on polished leaves. Hardy to 0°F. Partial or full shade. Moderate to regular water.

Japanese maple
*Acer palmatum**

This small deciduous tree is exceptionally graceful. Scores of varieties offer many choices in leaf shape and color. Overall shape is upright or mounding, depending on variety. Hardy to −10°F. Full sun or partial shade. Moderate to regular water.

Japanese snowdrop tree
Styrax japonicus

In spring, fragrant white flowers hang from strongly horizontal branches of this elegant deciduous tree. Hardy to −10°F, it can reach 30 ft. high and wide. Full sun or partial shade. Regular water.

Redbud
Cercis

With early spring flowers, colorful summer foliage, bright fall color, and interesting winter seedpods, these deciduous shrubs and small trees are truly all-season performers. Hardiness and water needs depend on type. Full sun or light shade.

Shrubby cinquefoil
*Potentilla fruticosa**

Tough enough to survive −40°F, this deciduous shrub offers blooms of white, yellow, pink, or orange to red over a long season. Most varieties grow 2–4 ft. tall and 2–5 ft. wide. Full sun. Moderate water.

*Good in containers

OTHER GREAT CHOICES
Flowering crabapple *Malus*
Japanese aralia *Fatsia japonica**
Japanese tree lilac *Syringa reticulata*
Kousa dogwood *Cornus kousa*
Lily-of-the-valley shrub *Pieris japonica**
Trident maple *Acer buergeranum**

Hillside Heroes

Refashion a sloping lawn or neglected bank with plants that control erosion and thrive on an incline.

Bearberry
Arctostaphylos uva-ursi

Flat-growing evergreen shrub can spread to 15 ft. Bright green leaves, pink to white flowers, and glowing red berries guarantee year-round appeal. Hardy to −50°F. Full sun or light shade. Little to moderate water.

Common ninebark
Physocarpus opulifolius

Great for tough spots where less durable plants fail, this deciduous shrub reaches 9 ft. tall and 10 ft. wide. Arching branches carry white or pinkish flowers. Red- and golden-leafed varieties are available. Survives −40°F. Sun or shade. Moderate to regular water.

Cotoneaster

Spreading form makes it ideal for slopes. Look for cranberry cotoneaster (*Cotoneaster apiculatus*), 3 ft. tall and 4 ft. wide, and rock cotoneaster (*C. horizontalis*), 2–3 ft. tall and 15 ft. wide. Both offer small red fruits and survive −20°F. Full sun. Little to moderate water.

Euonymus fortunei

Choose prostrate forms of this evergreen shrub, which grow to 2 ft. high and spread to 8 ft. or wider. Common winter creeper (*Euonymus fortunei radicans*) grows 1 ft. high and spreads indefinitely. Hardy to −20°F. Sun or shade. Moderate to regular water.

Juniper
Juniperus

These needle-leafed evergreen shrubs are old favorites for tough gardening situations. Choose sprawling types as ground covers or

larger ones as hillside anchors. Several colors available. Many species hardy to −40°F. Full sun or partial shade. Little to moderate water.

Lavender cotton
Santolina chamaecyparissus

Whitish gray leaves form a mound 2 ft. tall and 3 ft. wide; yellow buttonlike flowers are an added bonus. This tough plant thrives in hot spots and makes an excellent accent or ground cover. Hardy to −10°F. Full sun. Little to moderate water.

Siberian carpet cypress
Microbiota decussata

This sprawling evergreen shrub is unfazed by cold to −40°F. Handsome green needlelike foliage takes on dark red or purple tones in winter. Grows 1½ ft. tall and 8 ft. wide. Full sun or partial shade. Moderate water.

Switch grass
Panicum virgatum

Beautifully bold ornamental grass with green to blue-green leaves that turn red or yellow in fall. Airy flowers reach 7 ft. tall. Leaves and flowers change to beige in winter, but still look striking. Hardy to −40°F. Full sun or light shade. Moderate water.

Wisteria

Usually seen growing on trellises or arbors, this popular vine also makes a good bank cover; look for well-behaved species. Large leaves are a fresh green; spectacular clusters of springtime flowers are blue, white, or pink. Good choices are American wisteria (*Wisteria frutescens*) and its cousin Kentucky wisteria (*W. macrostachya*), both hardy to −10°F. Full sun. Little to moderate water.

Water Wise

Plant these perennial favorites to change a traditional thirsty garden into a drought-tolerant showcase.

Agastache

Spiky blooms in pink, purple, blue, red, or orange are held above mounds of fragrant leaves in summer; blooms attract hummingbirds. Hardiest types survive to −10°F. Several can be grown as annuals. Full sun or partial shade. Moderate water.

Artemisia

Look for types with soft, lacy, silvery white foliage. *Artemisia* 'Powis Castle' forms a dome to 3 ft. tall and a bit wider and is hardy to 0°F. *A. stellerana* 'Silver Brocade' is less than half as large and survives −40°F. Full sun. Little to moderate water.

Beard tongue
Penstemon

Beloved by gardeners and hummingbirds for spikes of blooms in white and many shades of red to blue. Most types are under 3 ft. tall; hardiness varies. Full sun or light shade. Little to moderate water.

Lamb's ears
Stachys byzantina

Ground-hugging plant with woolly, gray leaves delightfully soft to the touch—perfect for edging a path or flower bed. Interesting purple flowers in late spring or summer. Full sun or light shade. Moderate water.

Mexican daisy
Erigeron karvinskianus

Dainty white to pink daisylike flowers cover graceful trailing stems. Vigorous grower reaches 20 in. high and 3 ft. wide. Great

spilling onto paths or from containers. Hardy to −20°F. Full sun or light shade. Little to moderate water.

Muhlenbergia

Handsome grasses with narrow leaves in mounds to 5 ft. tall and 6 ft. wide in the largest types. Airy yellow, pink, or purple flower spikes hover on slender stems. Hardiness varies. Full sun. Little to moderate water.

Purple fountain grass
Pennisetum setaceum 'Rubrum'

Stunning as an accent, this variety forms a 5-ft. clump of burgundy-red leaves topped in summer by rose-colored plumes that slowly fade to beige. Survives 20°F; often grown as an annual. Full sun. Little to moderate water.

Russian sage
Perovskia

Blooms like a purple cloud. Tiny flowers float above a 3- to 4-ft. mass of grayish white stems and gray-green leaves. Hardy to −30°F and ideal for hot-summer regions. Full sun. Little to moderate water.

Stonecrop
Sedum

Among the hardiest are low-growing types such as *S. spurium* and *S. kamtschaticum*. They make a spreading carpet of small, thick leaves, sometimes variegated, topped in summer by pink or yellow flowers. Both species survive −30°F. Full sun or partial shade. Little to moderate water.

OTHER GREAT CHOICES
Catmint *Nepeta × faassenii*
Coreopsis
Cupid's dart *Catananche caerulea*
Santolina
Wild indigo *Baptisia*
Yarrow *Achillea*

Bog Beauties

Re-imagine a difficult boggy area as an opportunity for abundance.

Cardinal flower
Lobelia cardinalis

Brilliant scarlet flowers on upright spikes have made this a longtime favorite perennial for damp spots. Reaches 3–4 ft. high and blooms in summer. Hardy to −40°F. Full sun or partial shade. Ample water.

Dwarf purple osier
Salix purpurea 'Nana'

Makes a subtle color statement with blue-green leaves and slender purple branches. This appealing small shrub is just right for a clipped hedge 1–3 ft. tall. Hardy to −40°F. Full sun. Regular to ample water.

Globeflower
Trollius

In spring or summer, rich yellow to orange flowers rise 2–3 ft. above shiny, dark green leaves. Great cut flowers. Hardy to −20°F, this perennial grows best in cool-summer climates. Full sun or partial shade. Regular to ample water.

Iris (beardless)

This group contains many water-loving perennials, such as Japanese, Louisiana, and Siberian irises, all available in a dizzying array of colors. Other safe bets are yellow flag (*Iris pseudacorus*), blue flag (*I. versicolor*), and *I. laevigata*. Hardiness and exposure needs vary with type. Ample water.

Ligularia

Big, bold perennial forms a mass of leaves, each up to a foot wide. In summer, spikes of bright yellow or orange flowers rise as high as 6 ft. *Ligularia stenocephala* 'The Rocket' has stunning yellow flowers. Hardy to −30°F. Partial or full shade. Ample water.

Primrose
Primula japonica

Presents clusters of dainty flowers in purple, red, pink, or white in late spring to early summer. Blooms are held about 2 ft. above rosettes of light green leaves. This hardy perennial survives −40°F. Partial shade. Ample water.

Queen of the prairie
Filipendula rubra

In full bloom, this imposing perennial can reach 8 ft. tall and 4 ft. wide. Fluffy plumes of tiny pink flowers are eye-catching in summer, and they last a long time. Survives −40°F. Full sun or partial shade. Ample water.

Sweet flag
Acorus

Fountains of narrow, arching leaves are striped white or yellow in many types. Japanese sweet flag (*A. gramineus*) grows to about 1 ft. and is hardy to 0°F. *A. calamus* reaches 5 ft. tall and survives −30°F. Full sun or light shade. Ample water.

Turtlehead
Chelone lyonii

Glossy leaves form a good-looking low clump in spring and summer. From late summer to fall, these are topped with fascinating flowers of rose pink. Hardy to −40°F. Full sun or light shade. Ample water.

Virginia sweetspire
Itea virginica

This easy-to-grow deciduous shrub sports arching branches of rich green leaves; fragrant, creamy white flowers in summer are held in erect or drooping clusters to 6 in. long. Hardy to −10°F. Full sun or partial shade. Regular water.

Tropical Tone

Change an ordinary garden into a tropical paradise with these lush, showy plants.

Angel's trumpet
Brugmansia

Huge, fragrant, trumpet-shaped flowers in a range of warm colors hang from arching branches. Broad leaves to 2 ft. long. Hardiness varies, but most types can be grown in a container and moved indoors in winter. Sun or shade. Regular water.

Cast-iron plant
Aspidistra elatior

Its name indicates its toughness: this foliage plant thrives indoors or out. Glossy dark green leaves reach 2½ ft. long and are the perfect backdrop for colorful annuals. Hardy to 0°F. Partial or full shade. Moderate to regular water.

Common trumpet creeper
Campsis radicans

Deciduous vine grows to 40 ft., clinging to walls or fences. Bears 3-in. trumpet flowers of orange and scarlet. To −20°F. Full sun or partial shade. Moderate to regular water.

Five-finger fern
Adiantum aleuticum

Fresh and airy looking, this hardy little fern with its fingerlike fronds adds a touch of softness at the base of taller plants. The dark and wiry stems are lined with finely cut leaves. Grows to about 2 ft. tall and spreads slowly. Survives −40°F. Partial or full shade. Ample water.

Giant Burmese honeysuckle
Lonicera hildebrandiana

Train this fast-growing (to 30 ft.) deciduous vine against a warm wall or fence, or along eaves. White flowers reach 7 in. long and slowly turn yellow, then orange. Hardy to −10°F. Full sun or partial shade. Moderate to regular water.

Hercules' club
Aralia spinosa

Boasting huge leaves divided into many leaflets, white flowers, and purplish fruit, this small deciduous tree may reach 30 ft. tall and about half as wide. Despite its tropical appearance, it is hardy to −30ºF. Full sun or partial shade. Moderate to regular water.

Hosta

This popular broad-leafed perennial is available in a range of colors, shapes, and sizes. Look for varieties with deep green, blue, or chartreuse leaves; many are variegated with white, cream, or yellow. Summer white or lavender flowers are a bonus. Hardy to −40°F. Partial or full shade. Regular water.

Lily-of-the-Nile
Agapanthus

Masses of small blue or white flowers cluster at the tips of attractive green stems that may reach 5 ft. tall. Fountainlike foliage gives a lush, tropical feel—even without flowers. Some types are hardy to −10°F. Full sun or partial shade. Little to regular water.

Needle palm
Rhapidophyllum hystrix

This compact palm grows slowly to about 8 ft. tall and wide, displaying dramatic, dark green leaves to 3 ft. wide. Surviving 0°F, it is one of the hardiest palms available. Sun or shade. Moderate to ample water.

Sago palm
Cycas revoluta

Excellent in containers that can be brought indoors when temperatures drop below 15°F. Dark green feathery leaves grow from a central crown; looks like a small, primitive palm. Partial shade. Regular water.

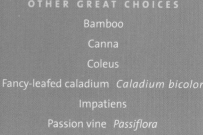

OTHER GREAT CHOICES

Bamboo

Canna

Coleus

Fancy-leafed caladium *Caladium bicolor*

Impatiens

Passion vine *Passiflora*

Late-Season Stars

Extend the garden's showy season with deciduous trees and shrubs that look great in fall and winter.

Dogwood
Cornus

Many dogwoods show beautiful color in fall; a few are also dramatic in winter. Cornelian cherry *(C. mas)* also bears red or yellow leaves and bright red berries in autumn; flaking bark is striking in winter. Cold-hardy redtwig dogwood *(C. stolonifera)* has red fall foliage and scarlet winter twigs. Full sun or light shade. Regular water.

Japanese barberry
Berberis thunbergii

These 4- to 6-ft. shrubs offer good fall color with small leaves adorning gracefully arching branches. Bright red berries are showy in autumn and winter. Hardy to −20°F. Full sun or light shade. Moderate to regular water.

Juneberry
Amelanchier

Fiery fall color, attractive bark, and an elegant winter silhouette make these large shrubs and small trees valuable additions to the year-round garden. Hardiness varies with type, but all appreciate a definite winter chill. Full sun or partial shade. Moderate to regular water.

Kerria japonica

This graceful 6-ft. shrub offers good-looking yellow foliage in autumn. In winter, branches remain yellowish to bright green and are excellent for flower arrangements. Hardy to −30°F. Partial sun. Moderate to regular water.

Larch
Larix

These tall trees have needlelike leaves that turn brilliant yellow and orange in fall. Small cones give leafless branches a polka-dot appearance in winter. Best in cool-summer regions with cool to cold winters. European larch *(L. decidua)* is hardy to −40°F. Full sun. Regular water.

Maidenhair tree
Ginkgo biloba

Distinctive silhouette and furrowed gray bark are attractive in winter, but the real show comes in fall, when leaves suddenly turn gold before dropping cleanly. Grows to 35–50 ft. tall. Plant only male trees. Hardy to −20°F. Full sun. Moderate to regular water.

Paperbark maple
Acer griseum

Perhaps the best of the many maples with beautiful fall color and interesting, colorful bark. This species grows to 25 ft. tall and is hardy to −30°F. Leaves turn brilliant red in autumn. Reddish bark peels off like sheets of paper. Full sun or partial shade. Moderate to regular water.

Persian parrotia
Parrotia persica

Autumn leaves of this 15- to 25-ft. shrubby tree turn golden, then orange to pink, and finally scarlet. Handsome gray bark peels off to show colorful patches, and red flowers appear in late winter to early spring. Survives −30°F. Full sun or light shade. Moderate to regular water.

Sourwood
Oxydendrum arboreum

A graceful flowering tree with rich green leaves that change to orange, scarlet, and deep purple in the fall. Typically grows 30–50 ft. tall and has a pyramidal shape and slightly drooping branches that make for a stunning winter silhouette. Hardy to −20°F. Full sun. Regular water.

Witch hazel
Hamamelis

These medium-size to large shrubs have autumn foliage in sizzling shades of yellow, orange, and red. Zigzagging branches make an appealing composition in winter, when fragrant yellow or red flowers appear in nodding clusters. Hardiness varies; some types survive −40°F. Full sun or partial shade. Regular water.

Index

Credits

Photography

Photographs are listed sequentially either in horizontal or vertical order. For additional clarification, the following position indicators may be used: Left (L), Center (C), Right (R), Top (T), Middle (M), Bottom (B).

Jean Allsopp: front sleeve; 40; 73BR; 136

Joyce Baker: 98

Paul Bousquet: 46T

Marion Brenner: 3; 4T; 6TR, MR, BR; 7BL,TR, BR; 9; 10; 12T; 13; 15T, B; 16; 17BL, BR; 18L; 19; 21; 22; 23; 24; 25B; 26; 27BL, BM, BR; 28T; 29; 30; 31T; 33; 34; 35R; 36R; 37; 43L; 49; 50; 51; 52; 53; 54TR, BR; 55; 68; 77; 78; 79; 80; 81; 88; 89; 90T; 93; 95; 96; 97TL, TR, BR; 107; 108; 110TR, BR; 111; 118; 119; 120R; 121; 130; 149TR; 150T; 151; 152B; 153T; 154T; 156B; back cover left A, B, bottom A, C

Steven Bue and Trish Dilworth-Bue: 70

James Carrier: 137

Van Chaplin: 73L; 112; 113; 116; 117; 142; 143

Glenn Christiansen: 44

Claire Curran: 125B

Robin B. Cushman: 83; 99; 102B; 105L

Janet Davis: 155T

Cynthia Del Fava: 6BL; 28B; 31B; 56; 62; 76; 84; 94; 110L

Alan and Linda Detrick: 73TR; 101BL

Derek Fell: 150B; 157T

Roger Foley: 115; 155B

Steven Gunther: 101TR; 124

Philip Harvey: 75T

Saxon Holt: 71; 105TR; 128B; 133; 149BL; 152T; 156T; back cover TR

Allan Mandell: 100; 125T; 128T; back cover bottom B

Charles Mann: 38; 39; 42; 43TR, BR; 45BL; 72; 102T; 103L, BR; 104; 129B; back cover bottom D

Tom Mannion: 114

Rod McLellan Company: 18R

Joyce Mixer: 82

Terrence Moore: 45T

Jerry Pavia: 101BR; 105BR; 127L, BR; 129T

Norman A. Plate: 4B; 5T, M; 7ML, MR; 11TR; 14; 91; 97BL; 109T; 122; 123; 126; 127TR; 132; 134; 135; 141; 144; back sleeve

Matthew Plut: 47

Susan A. Roth: 75B; 103TR

Greg Ryan/Sally Beyer: 148

Christina Schmidhofer: 74

Thomas J. Story: 1; 4M; 6TL, ML; 8; 11TL, BL, BR; 15M; 17TL; 20; 45BR; 48; 57; 58; 59; 60; 61; 63; 65; 66; 67; 69; 85T; 86; 87TM, BL, BR; 90B; 138; 139; 140; 145; 146

Southern Progress Corporation: 5B; 27T; 41; 154B; 157B

Scott Terry: 92

Michael S. Thompson: 153B

Tom Wilhite: 7TL; 12B; 25T; 32; 36L; 54L; 106; 120L

Tom Woodward: 35L; 87TR

Design

Linda Applewhite & Associates: 74

Jeff Bale: 128T

Shari Bashin-Sullivan: 71

Bob Clark: 7BL; 153T

Jim Cohen: 103B

Jodie Collins: 27T

Connie Cross: 75B

Cynthia Del Fava: 66

Don Del Fava: 63

Topher Delaney: 44

Steve Fidrych: 12T; 15B; 43L; 50; 90; 97T, B

Rachel Foster: 83; 99

Nancy Hammer: 125T

Little & Lewis: 127TR

Steven R. Lorton: 123

David Lovro: 102T

David Mandel: 93

Tom Mannion: 115

Jim McCann: 69

Louise Mercer: 103TR

Carrie Nimmer: 39

J. Dabney Peebles Design Assoc.: 117

Jim Ripley: 134

Tina Rousselot: 102T

Sally Sheklow: 102B; 105L

Jill Slater: 11BR; 16; 68; 145

Bud Stuckey: 69; 139

Richard and Shari Sullivan: 47

Freeland Tanner: 152T

Terry Welch: 100

Peter O. Whiteley: 134; 146

Acknowledgments

Our thanks to the following people and businesses for their valuable advice and assistance:

Skip Antonelli, Antonelli Brothers Begonia Gardens, Santa Cruz, CA; Chuck Arnott, San Lorenzo Lumber Company Garden Center, Santa Cruz, CA; Cobblestone Antiques, Soquel, CA; Cottura, Palo Alto, CA; Casper R. Curto, Casper Landscape Design, Oakland, CA; Don Del Fava; Dressler Stencil Company, Renton, WA; Steve Fidrych; Eric and Ellen Gil, Warmth Company, Aptos, CA; Jennifer Greer; Charlotte Hagood; Mark Helme, Davenport, CA; Mark Henry, Santa Cruz Ground Cover, Santa Cruz, CA; Nancy Howell; Louis Joyner; Pier 1 Imports, Redwood City, CA; The Potting Shed, Fairfax, CA; Redwood City Nursery, Redwood City, CA; Roger Reynolds Nursery, Menlo Park, CA; Cathy Ritter, Safe & Beautiful Trees & Landscape, Mountain View, CA; Terrie Scott; Sloat Garden Center, Kentfield, CA; Vicky Smith, Victoria's Orchids, Santa Cruz, CA; James Stolley, Jr.; Victor Thomas, Lyngso Garden Materials, Redwood City, CA; Smith & Hawken, Palo Alto, CA; Julia Hamilton Thomason; Tiffany's Antiques, Santa Cruz, CA; Jose Villalpando, Jose Garden Service, San Mateo, CA; Wisteria Antiques & Design, Soquel, CA

We also extend our appreciation to the following individuals for their support: Steve Baumhoff; Bridget and Kirk Bradley; Leon and Mary Louise Fidrych; Alice Jordan; the Library Staff of Southern Progress Corporation; Audrey Mak; Ed and Flora Rogers; Linda J. Selden; Janet Jungnick Smith; Fred Taylor

Page 48: Excerpt from THE INVITING GARDEN by Allen Lacy ©1998 by Allen Lacy. Reprinted by permission of Henry Holt and Company, LLC